A Dictionary of
THE BATTLE OF BRITAIN

A Dictionary of

THE BATTLE
OF BRITAIN

IN ASSOCIATION WITH THE BATTLE OF BRITAIN MEMORIAL TRUST

GEOFF SIMPSON

HALSGROVE

First published in Great Britain in 2009
Reprinted 2010

Copyright © Geoff Simpson 2009

Published by Halsgrove in Association with
The Battle of Britain Memorial Trust

British Library Cataloguing-in-Publication Data
A CIP record for this title is available from the British Library

ISBN 978 1 84114 982 0

HALSGROVE
Halsgrove House,
Ryelands Industrial Estate,
Bagley Road, Wellington, Somerset TA21 9PZ
Tel: 01823 653777   Fax: 01823 216796
email: sales@halsgrove.com

Part of the Halsgrove group of companies
Information on all Halsgrove titles is available at: www.halsgrove.com

Printed and bound in Great Britain by The Cromwell Press Group, Wiltshire

CONTENTS

ACKNOWLEDGEMENTS

The author gratefully acknowledges the help of the following in the preparation of this book:

Victoria Thompson has been a knowledgeable, enthusiastic and assiduous part time research assistant.

The Trustees of the Battle of Britain Memorial Trust have been most encouraging and helpful, notably, the President, Air Chief Marshal Sir Michael Graydon, GCB, CBE, the Chairman, Richard Hunting and the Secretary, Group Captain Patrick Tootal, OBE, DL.

Over more than 20 years many others have helped me as I tried to understand the events of 1940. Sadly, a considerable number of those in the lists that follow have since died.

Above all, I have had the privilege of meeting and corresponding with several hundred of "The Few". Amongst those with whom I have conducted detailed conversations and correspondence are: Squadron Leader D L Armitage, DFC; Squadron Leader C S Bamberger, DFC*, AE*; Squadron Leader P P C Barthropp, DFC, AFC; Flight Lieutenant L G Batt; Squadron Leader R A Beardsley, DFC; Wing Commander H J S Beazley, DFC; Air Commodore P M Brothers, CBE, DSO, DFC*; Flight Lieutenant O V Burns; Wing Commander I H Cosby, DFC; Wing Commander E C Deanesly, DFC; Warrant Officer H D Denchfield; Air Vice-Marshal R D Deacon-Elliott, DFC; Group Captain B Drake, DSO, DFC; Group Captain J Ellis, CBE, DFC*; Air Commodore J N W Farmer, DFC; Flying Officer R V Forward; Wing Commander R W Foster, DFC, AE; Air Chief Marshal Sir Christopher Foxley-Norris, GCB, DSO, OBE; Sqn Ldr C G Frizell; Group Captain T P Gleave CBE; Group Captain E Graham; Flight Lieutenant R H D Hall, DFC; Squadron Leader R F Hamlyn AFC, DFM; Wing Commander N P W Hancock, OBE, DFC; Wing Commander R E Havercroft, AFC; Squadron Leader T C Iveson, DFC, AE; Air Vice Marshal J E Johnson, CB, CBE, DSO**, DFC*; Flight Lieutenant R L Jones; Squadron Leader A C Leigh, DFC, DFM; Squadron Leader K R Lusty; Flt Lt R C Nutter, DFC; Wing Commander A G Page, DSO, OBE, DFC*; Wing Commander P L Parrot, DFC*, AFC; Squadron Leader T G Pickering; Flight Lieutenant N H D Ramsay, DFC; Flight Lieutenant D N Robinson; Flight Lieutenant L E Hooper-Smith, AE; Wing Commander J E Storrar, DFC*; Wing Commander J A Thomson; Flight Lieutenant W L B Walker, AE; Group Captain A R Wright, DFC*, AFC; Wing Commander J R C Young, AFC.

Close family members of the following of The Few have also kindly submitted to detailed questioning. + = lost in the Battle.

Sgt E S Bann+; Plt Off N J V Benson+; Sgt G B Booth+; Fg Off P E G Carter+; Plt Off H A Case+; Sgt F W Eley*; Flt Lt K L Gillies+; Sgt W B Higgins+; Plt Off R M Hogg+; Wg Cdr D E Kingaby; DSO, AFC, DFM**; Air Cdre A R D MacDonell, CB, DFC; Sgt P R C McIntosh+; Plt Off G H Maffett+; Fg Off H K F Matthews+; Plt Off H W Reilley+; Plt Off D C Shepley+; Sgt R A Ward+; Sgt B E P Whall, DFM+; Plt Off C A Woods-Scawen, DFC+; Fg Off P P Woods-Scawen+, DFC; Wg Cdr R D Yule, DSO, DFC*.

Most helpful too were other people who participated in, or witnessed, the events and personalities of 1940. They include: Kath Baldwin; "Joe" Crawshaw; Sydney Cripps; "Bunny" Ford; Geoffrey Goodman, CBE, DFC; Lord Graham of Edmonton PC; Les Hayes; Jimmy Hensler; Bert Hooker; Major Gerald Jackson MC; Lord Jenkins of Hillhead OM, PC; Charlotte Lill; The Second Lord Newall; Wg Cdr Alan Newitt, DFC; Avis Parsons, MM; Ray Reason; Joyce and Jack Simpson; John Virgo; Colin Ward, DFM.

Historians, authors and researchers who have been generous in sharing their knowledge include: Bryan Badham; Paul Beaver; Wing Commander Tom Barrett; Peter Bebbington; Derek Boughton; D L Bradley; Colin Brown; David Brocklehurst; Dr Stephen Bungay; Ian Burrows; Chris Chandler; Flight Lieutenant Roy Chapman; Laurie Chester; John Coleman; Jarrod Cotter; Dr Jeremy Crang; Philip Curtis; Ken Daniels; Fred Dunster; Barry Fletcher; Michael Ginns, MBE; Gary Godel; Roy Goodey; "Dan" Gurney; Group Captain John Hollowood; Peter Knottley; Michael Korda; Roger Lewis; Dr Peter H Liddle; Michael Long; Edward McManus; Sean Maffett; Stephanie Maltman; Dr Tony Mansell; Bob Ogley; Air Commodore Graham Pitchfork, MBE; Dr Alfred Price; John Richards; R C Riley; Dr Sebastian Ritchie; Rob Rooker; David Ross; Alan Savage, MBE; James Siddelley; Leonard G Smith; Malcolm Smith, MBE; John Sutton; Anthony Tuck; Kenneth G Wynn.

FOREWORD

With perhaps a third of the population of this country over 60 years old, the Battle of Britain still has real meaning, either as a result of personal memory or through hearing parents or relatives recall the time when Britain stood alone. Or, they will have seen films such as Angels One Five or the iconic Battle of Britain movie made in the 1960s.

These generations will know a good deal about this epic battle. But, memories are not flawless, details are forgotten and the mind needs a jog to get it moving. This book will do just that. "Why were the encounters called dog fights?" "Was the Spitfire better than the Bf 109?" It is all here.

So, much of the population can be reminded of 1940 with some ease. But there are generations now who, sadly, know all too little about this event.

The Battle of Britain Memorial Trust intends to change this deficiency. At Capel-le-Ferne, where the National Memorial stands, the Trust will create a visual history lesson; it plans to reproduce a dispersal hut from where the pilots scrambled to engage the enemy, a film will explain the Battle and its importance; and it will provide an opportunity for the younger generation to relive a moment in time when the world watched with bated breath. And, they too, this younger generation, our future, will have at hand this book to guide them through this pivotal period of the 20th century and the foundation of their freedom today.

Read it. Remind yourself. Learn and speak thereafter with pride and knowledge of the men and women who fought in the Battle of Britain.

Air Chief Marshal Sir Michael Graydon, GCB, CBE
President
Battle of Britain Memorial Trust

Our Wall

A poem written by Flt Lt William Walker with Capel-le-Ferne in mind

Here inscribed the names of friends we knew,

Young men with whom we often flew,

Scrambled to many angels high

They knew that they or friends might die.

Many were very scarcely trained

And many badly burnt or maimed,

Behind each name a story lies

Of bravery in summer skies.

Though many brave unwritten tales

Were simply told in vapour trails,

Many now lie in sacred graves

And many rest beneath the waves;

Outnumbered every day they flew

Remembered here as just "The Few"

In 1940 Plt Off Walker was a Spitfire pilot with No 616 (South Yorkshire) Squadron. On August 26, at about noon, he baled out wounded into the sea off Dover and was rescued by the Royal Navy.

A MESSAGE FROM WING COMMANDER BOB FOSTER, DFC, AE

CHAIRMAN, BATTLE OF BRITAIN FIGHTER ASSOCIATION

I very much enjoyed leafing through this book as it rekindled vivid memories of those hot and hectic summer days of 1940.

The code words are all too familiar. For instance the sequence of:-

"Turkey Squadron scramble – vector 120 angels 20".

And later "Blue 2 to Leader, Bandits 10 o'clock low 50 plus."

Leader – "I see them, Turkey Squadron Battle formation Go."

Then maybe – Yellow 3 (weaving behind the Squadron) "Beware the high squadron possible 'Snappers', 2 o'clock high."

Ignore them and into the bombers for better or for worse.

I was also pleased to see reference to the Auxiliary Squadrons and the VR. Had it not been for the foresight of Trenchard and others in the 1920 and 30s in forming these reserves the Battle may well have been lost.

Fighter Command had taken a caning against heavy odds in France and over Dunkirk that it was only the timely arrival of the reserve forces that brought the squadrons back to operational and fighting strength in August and September. Even so it was touch and go for a time.

Credit must also be given to the men from the Commonwealth, the Poles, Czechs, Americans and others who together with the Royal Air Force inflicted the first defeat on Nazi Germany.

The debt this country and indeed the World owes should never be forgotten.

In 1940 Plt Off Foster flew Hurricanes with No 605 (County of Warwick) Squadron.

THE NATIONAL MEMORIAL

Many years after the Second World War the idea of a National Memorial to the Allied airmen who flew in the Battle of Britain was conceived.

The plan came from Wg Cdr Geoffrey Page who had been a 20-year-old Hurricane pilot in the Battle with No 56 Squadron. On August 12 1940 Plt Off Page found himself fighting to escape from a burning Hurricane off the Kent coast.

He eventually did so and then struggled to open his parachute because his hands were so badly burned. Having overcome that problem too, he was rescued from the sea and soon became a patient at the Queen Victoria Hospital, East Grinstead, in the care of the surgeon Archibald McIndoe. In 1941 he was a founder member of The Guinea Pig Club.

Geoffrey returned to action and became a Wing Leader, winning the DSO, DFC and bar. In 1944 he crashed on landing, fracturing his back and damaging his face on the aircraft's gunsight. He returned to East Grinstead.

When Geoffrey realised that there was no national memorial to his comrades in 1940 he established the Battle of Britain Memorial Trust to put things right.

His vision led to the moment on July 9 1993, when Her Late Majesty, Queen Elizabeth the Queen Mother unveiled the National Memorial to The Few at Capel-le-Ferne, on the cliffs between Folkestone and Dover.

Today the Memorial Trust continues to run the Memorial site, which also now features replicas of a Hurricane and a Spitfire from the Battle and the Christopher Foxley-Norris Memorial Wall on which are inscribed the names of all the allied aircrew who qualified for the "immediate" award of the 1939-45 Star, with Battle of Britain clasp.

The Trust is always seeking funds to maintain and develop the National Memorial, so that future generations will learn of the heroism displayed by so many in 1940 at a turning point in British history.

Further information can be obtained from: www.battleofbritainmemorial.org.uk

INTRODUCTION

To grow up in south east London in the 1950s was to learn about the war and the Battle of Britain in particular, without effort or realisation. Almost anyone who was a few years older had witnessed the Battle from the ground – there were tales of being bombed out, of anti-aircraft shrapnel coming through the roof, of the Spitfire that crashed on Woolwich Common and the Messerschmitt that fell in Plumstead.

There were the scars and souvenirs of wartime too. The "bomb sites", the damage to buildings, the prefabs and the people whose appearance or behaviour demanded an explanation of their wartime experiences. People might still announce that they would "black out" rather than draw the curtains and a person who was over excited or eccentric might still be described as "bomb happy".

In 1940 the people of London and south east England had been at the ringside at a turning point in history. Indeed, they had all played their part too. Britain might have been invaded and subjugated, but it was not. That possibility was ended by the efforts of many people, military and civilian. The men who flew into action overhead rightly received the highest share of the credit, but, as I have discovered since, "The Few" are keen to share the approbation. They could not have done without those who cheered them on and, often, aided their efforts.

This book is one more tribute to all those men and women who stood together in 1940.

The Battle of Britain Memorial Trust hopes that it will be of use to researchers, but also attractive to people with a general interest in the events of the summer and autumn of that year.

The Trust believes it is vital that the story of the time, within living memory, when Britain faced invasion should be told again and again, so that future generations learn of the heroism of so many people both service and civilian.

Inevitably, the story is recounted here mainly from the British perspective. Interleaved with the bare facts of the great air battle that was fought over this country are the human stories and the trivia that remain in the minds of those who were there.

Geoff Simpson
April 3 2009

AUTHOR'S NOTE

There are no entries for individual members of "The Few". It would be inappropriate to pick out just some and biographical notes on all of them appear in *Men of the Battle of Britain* by Kenneth G Wynn. Equally, the equipment, locations and activities of individual squadrons are well chronicled elsewhere and any attempt to cover that ground here would greatly increase the length of the book.

The subject of wartime ranks is extremely complicated. Generally the ranks used are those in which the people concerned were operating at the time. No attempt has been made to differentiate between substantive, wartime substantive, temporary, acting or other classes of rank.

Where no year is given in a date, the reference is to 1940.

ABBREVIATIONS USED IN THIS BOOK

AA – Anti-Aircraft
AAF – Auxiliary Air Force
A/c - Aircraft
AC1 – Aircraftman First Class
ADC – Aide de Camp
AFC – Air Force Cross
AFM – Air Force Medal
AHB – Air Historical Branch
Air Cdre – Air Commodore
Air Chf Mshl – Air Chief Marshal
Air Mshl – Air Marshal
AOC – Air Officer Commanding
AO CinC – Air Officer, Commanding-in-Chief
ARP – Air Raid Precautions
ATA – Air Transport Auxiliary
ATC – Air Training Corps
ATS – Auxiliary Territorial Service
AVM – Air Vice Marshal
BBFA – Battle of Britain Fighter Association
CAS – Chief of the Air Staff
CFS – Central Flying School
CGC – Conspicuous Gallantry Cross
CGM – Conspicuous Gallantry Medal
CO – Commanding Officer
Cpl - Corporal
CWGC – Commonwealth War Graves Commission
DFC – Distinguished Flying Cross
DSC – Distinguished Service Cross
DSO – Distinguished Service Order
EGM – Empire Gallantry Medal
FAA – Fleet Air Arm
Fg Off – Flying Officer
GC – George Cross
Gp Capt – Group Captain
GOC – General Officer Commanding
HM – His Majesty
HQ – Headquarters
IWGC – Imperial War Graves Commission
IWM – Imperial War Museum

KCB - Knight Commander of the Order of the Bath
LAC – Leading Aircraftman
LDV – Local Defence Volunteers
LFB – London Fire Brigade
M o D – Ministry of Defence
MRAF – Marshal of the Royal Air Force
NCO – Non-Commissioned Officer
NZ – New Zealand
OC – Officer Commanding
OM – Order of Merit
OTU – Operational Training Unit
PC – Police Constable
Plt Off – Pilot Officer
PoW – Prisoner of War
RAE – Royal Aircraft Establishment
RAAF – Royal Australian Air Force
RAF – Royal Air Force
RAFO – Reserve of Air Force Officers
RAFVR – Royal Air Force Volunteer Reserve
R Aux A F – Royal Auxiliary Air Force
RCAF – Royal Canadian Air Force
RFC – Royal Flying Corps
RHA – Royal Horse Artillery
RMA – Royal Military Academy
RNAS – Royal Naval Air Service
RN – Royal Navy
RNLI – Royal National Lifeboat Institution
SASO – Senior Air Staff Officer
Sgt - Sergeant
Sqn Ldr – Squadron Leader
TA – Territorial Army
UN – United Nations
USAAF – United States Army Air Force
VC – Victoria Cross
WAAF – Women's Auxiliary Air Force
Wg Cdr – Wing Commander
WOP/AG – Wireless Operator/ Air Gunner
WVS – Women's Voluntary Service

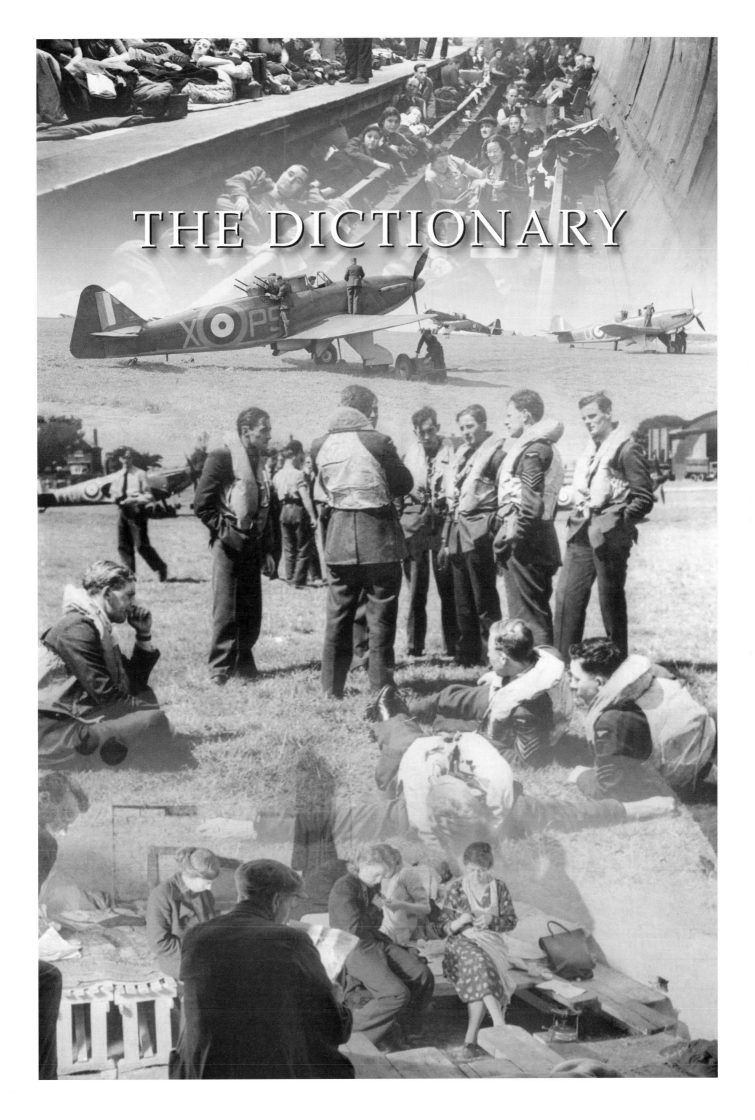

THE DICTIONARY

This Dornier of the Holzhammer Geschwader failed to return from Adler Tag. Attacked by at least two RAF fighters while bombing the airfield at Eastchurch, the aircraft came down at Paxton Farm, Stodmarsh, north east of Canterbury. The pilot, Unteroffizier Vogel and the rest of the crew were taken prisoner. (Kent Messenger PD1463476)

Ace – A term normally used in the RAF to denote a pilot who had achieved the destruction of five enemy aircraft in combat.

Adlerangriff (Eagle Attack) – German expression for the attacks which, if all went according to plan, would cripple Fighter Command as a prelude to invasion.

Adler Tag (Eagle Day) – The day on which Adlerangriff would be launched. Eventually this occurred on August 13, with the considerable deficiencies in German intelligence being a prime cause of its relative lack of success.

Air Transport Auxiliary – Organisation established in 1939 following a proposal by Gerard d'Erlanger, a director of the then British Airways – his original concept involved a pool of civilian pilots carrying out such duties as the ferrying of mail, medical and other light supplies and ambulance work. However, aircraft delivery soon became a major task.

Many ATA pilots were men considered unsuitable for RAF and FAA flying, through age or other cause. They were inclined to refer to themselves as "Ancient and Tattered Airmen".

A women's section, led by Pauline Gower, was established in 1940. Women flew all types of aircraft except amphibians off water. They also acted as flight engineers on four-engined aircraft such as the Avro Lancaster.

ATA personnel delivered Fairey Battles to France in May 1940, aircraft to Fighter Command airfields during the Battle of Britain and flew into Europe again after D-Day.

Before its disbandment at the end of the war the ATA had delivered 309,011 aircraft and suffered 174 aircrew deaths.

According to Lord Beaverbrook, "Without the ATA the days and nights of the Battle of Britain would have been conducted under conditions quite different from the actual events... They were soldiers fighting in the struggle just as completely as if they had been engaged on the battlefront."

Airfield Defence – The Army provided many of the troops to defend airfields against possible attempts by German parachute and glider-borne troops to capture them, although the RAF trade of Ground Gunner was created in 1940. Later the airfield defence role would normally be performed by the RAF Regiment, formed in 1942. Built defences at Battle of Britain airfields included both real and dummy pillboxes.

On August 18 at Kenley, Second Lieutenant Hague of the Scots Guards earned the MC and Lance Corporals Miller and Gale the MM. On the same day Private Joseph Lister of the

Border Regiment earned the MM at Manston. Despite severe wounds, which led to the loss of a leg, he continued to fire a Bren gun at Bf 109s strafing the airfield.

Anderson, Sir John (1882-1958) – A civil servant from 1905, who was said to have been deeply affected when handed a white feather by a woman when crossing Whitehall during the First World War. He subsequently volunteered for military service, but was not called up. In 1926, as Permanent Under Secretary at the Home Office, he attended daily cabinet committee meetings during the General Strike. It is alleged that at one meeting Winston Churchill advocated the use of armed troops to protect supplies of newsprint for the

Aldwych underground station in use as a shelter on October 8. (Courtesy of Imperial War Museum, London, negative number HU 44272)

A photograph taken in 1940 showing Alan and Doris Suter entering the Anderson shelter in the garden of their home at 44 Edgeworth Road, Eltham, London, in 1940. Their mother is behind them. Alan has his gas mask box. (Courtesy Imperial War Museum, London, negative number D 778)

government newspaper, *British Gazette.* Anderson's retort was, "I would beg the Chancellor of the Exchequer to stop talking nonsense."

From 1932 to 1937 Anderson was Governor of Bengal and survived two assassination attempts.

In 1938, as an independent, he won a Scottish Universities seat in Parliament in the bye-election caused by the death of Ramsay MacDonald. Shortly afterwards he was appointed Lord Privy Seal with the task of co-ordinating civil defence measures. He asked William Paterson, a friend, to design a small air raid shelter for families. The result was the "Anderson Shelter" in gardens, of which millions were produced.

On the outbreak of war Anderson became Minister of Home Security and an attendee at meetings of the War Cabinet. He remained in the post after Churchill became PM. Anderson was initially unhurried in his approach to the internment of enemy nationals, but, after a rebuke from Churchill and other criticism, he instigated a much tougher policy including the detention of some British nationals.

Anderson was adamant in not believing in the building of deep shelters, which he considered would be wasteful of men and materials and would create a "shelter mentality". After the mass bombing of London began on September 7 he was attacked in the press and in Parliament on this score. In October he was replaced at the Home Office by Herbert Morrison, seen as a more sure-footed Parliamentary performer. Anderson became Lord President of the Council, the only significant setback of his career. His disappointment was mitigated by being made a member of the War Cabinet.

In 1945 when Churchill and Eden were about to set off for the Yalta conference, Churchill wrote to the King advising him that, if both should be killed, Anderson should be sent for.

Anderson's post war appointments included the Chairmanship of the Port of London Authority. He left Parliament in 1950, when his seat was abolished and was created Viscount Waverley in 1952.

Angels – Height expressed in thousands of feet, so "Angels 15" would indicate 15,000ft. However, it became apparent that the enemy was making use of this information, so false figures were introduced; thus "Angels 18" might actually mean "21,000 ft" to the leader of a Fighter Command formation.

"Hello Short Jack, Tennis leader calling. Tennis squadron airborne, making Angels 20 – over." Extract from the script, prepared by officers who were involved in 1940, for a recreation on Horseguards Parade in September 1959. The leader of No 72, a Spitfire squadron, is depicted talking to the deputy controller at Biggin Hill as a raid approaches.

One of the best remembered films relating to the Battle is *Angels One Five* (1952), a fictional account of a pilot's life and death, with actors including John Gregson, Jack Hawkins, Michael Denison, Dulcie Gray, Cyril Raymond and Humphrey Lestocq.

Anti-Aircraft Command – Anti-aircraft fire shot down relatively few German aircraft, but did scatter formations and (together with searchlights) gave the public a clear demonstration that Britain was hitting back. Detritus from the barrage caused damage and casualties on the ground.

The Command was established on April 1 1939, initially under the command of General Sir Alan Brooke, though he quickly handed over to Lieutenant General Sir Frederick Pile, who would retain the post throughout the war.

In the latter part of the conflict the Command achieved notable successes against the V1 flying bombs.

Artists – In the early years of the war a number of artists were given official commissions to paint and draw Fighter Command aircrew. Captain Cuthbert Orde, for example, began work in September 1940. Helped by his First World War service in the RFC as an observer and test pilot, he seems to have empathised with his subjects and the nicknames he acquired included, "Turps" and "Uncle Orde". Some of his portraits appeared in *Pilots of Fighter Command* in 1942.

Battle of Britain by Paul Nash, painted in 1941. (Courtesy of Imperial War Museum, London, negative number LD 1550)

Others to do similar work included Eric Kennington and Sir William Rothenstein, both of whom had been official war artists in the First World War.

Eric Kennington, mainly a sculptor, had become well known for his painting *The Kensingtons at Laventie*, completed in 1916 and now in the IWM. It portrayed men of the 13th (County of London) Princess Louise's Kensington Battalion, including Kennington, immediately after leaving the front line.

Rothenstein had been arrested on the Western Front in the Great War as a suspected spy, his German name being the cause of the problem. In 1942 a number of his fighter pilot portraits appeared in *Men of the RAF*.

In 1941 Paul Nash painted *Battle of Britain*, a depiction of aerial combat as viewed from the ground. It is in the collection of the IWM.

Ashmore, Major General Edward Bailey (1872-1953) – Served with Royal Horse Artillery in the (second) Boer War, being badly wounded in the action at Sanna's (or

Sannah's) Post on March 31 1900 which resulted in five VCs, including four to the RHA.

On September 3 1912 he qualified as a pilot, gaining Royal Aero Club certificate no 281. In 1917, having commanded 4th Brigade, RFC during the Battle of the Somme (1916), he was appointed to set up an air defence system for London, establishing a balloon barrage and a gun belt 25 miles to the east of the capital, with fighters patrolling inside it. White arrows on the ground directed the fighters to incoming enemy aircraft. Ground observers were used as well as wireless-equipped tracker aircraft.

After Ashmore ceased to be GOC, London Air Defence Area in October 1918, his innovations were neglected, though he held various further posts in connection with home defence. His experiments with observer posts around Cranbrook, Kent in 1924 provided the origins of the Observer Corps. Overall, he can be said to be the instigator of what became known as the "Dowding System" of defence.

Ashmore retired in 1929. In 1940 he raised and commanded the 6th West Sussex Battalion, LDV.

"(Ashmore) is very often forgotten, but he was the first pioneer." Historian, Derek Wood, speaking at *The Battle Re-thought*, a symposium organised by the RAF Historical Society and the RAF Staff College, Bracknell, June 1990.

Auxiliary Air Force – Reserve organisation, with a territorial basis, intended to create an elite of young men. On September 12 1925 the formation began of the first squadron, 602 (City of Glasgow). On the outbreak of war, AAF personnel joined the RAFVR, "for the emergency". Fourteen pre-war AAF squadrons took park in the Battle of Britain. The organisation was re-established on June 2 1946 and granted permission to use the Royal prefix by King George VI on December 16 1947.

Disbandment occurred in June 1957, though the R Aux A F was later re-established.

Before the war a scheme was introduced to train AAF ground crew to become NCO pilots. Frederick Ernest Richard Shepherd of No 611 Squadron was accepted as a participant. After qualifying, Sgt Shepherd rejoined the squadron. On September 11, he baled out with his parachute on fire and fell dead at Frylands Wood, Farleigh, Surrey. His Spitfire crashed into houses in Hartland Way, Shirley, Croydon. Sgt Shepherd's front line career had lasted 10 days. He was buried amongst Fighter Command comrades in "Airmen's Corner" at St Luke's Churchyard, Whyteleafe, Surrey.

The AAF squadrons that took part in the Battle were:-

No 501 (County of Gloucester)

No 504 (City of Nottingham)

No 600 (City of London)

No 601 (County of London)

No 602 (City of Glasgow)

No 603 (City of Edinburgh)

No 604 (County of Middlesex)

No 605 (County of Warwick)

No 607 (County of Durham)

No 609 (West Riding of Yorkshire)

No 610 (County of Chester)

No 611 (West Lancashire)

No 615 (County of Surrey "Churchill's Own")

No 616 (South Yorkshire)

The future Prime Minister had become Honorary Air Cdre of 615 Squadron before the war.

Kite balloons rise above the airfield at Cardington, Bedfordshire, during handling practice by No 1 Balloon Training Unit, October 1940. Courtesy Imperial War Museum, London, negative number CH 1523)

Balloon Command – Balloons were used as a defensive measure against aircraft by both the British and the Germans in the Great War. Balloon Command was formed on November 1 1938 under the control of Fighter Command. When war came balloons directly downed few aircraft but helped to disperse formations and keep the enemy away from key targets. They were often regarded as targets of opportunity by the Luftwaffe and sometimes provided a spectacular show when they were shot up.

It appears that the first aircraft in the Second World War to fall victim to British balloons was a Hampden of No 106 Squadron on a night training flight in the Coventry area. This incident occurred on May 24 and the crew of Plt Off J M D Irvine, Sgt J R Collingham and AC1 S E Firth was killed.

From 1941 women steadily replaced men at balloon sites in the UK. The original formula that 20 WAAFs were required to replace 10 male operators was reduced to a 14:10 ratio.

Balloon Command was disbanded in February 1945.

Bandits – Identified enemy aircraft.

Battle of the Barges – Name applied to the attacks by Bomber and Coastal Commands on the river barges being assembled across the Channel, as part of the German preparations for invasion. From the beginning of July missions were flown, with heavy losses, against barge concentrations in such locations as Le Havre, Boulogne, Dunkirk, Ostend, Antwerp and the Dortmund-Ems canal.

Battle of Britain Day – Each year September 15 is marked as Battle of Britain Day. On a weekend after that date the BBFA holds its annual general meeting and a service of commemoration is held in Westminster Abbey, a tradition dating back to 1944.

In 1940 September 15 was a Sunday on which the RAF and the Luftwaffe fought on a large scale over London and south east England. Though the German casualties were nowhere near what was alleged at the time (185 claimed, about one third of which represented the true figure), the Luftwaffe suffered a major setback that day. In retrospect this can be argued to be the climactic moment of the Battle.

Wg Cdr Bob Foster (left), who became Chairman of the BBFA in early 2009, photographed at a House of Commons reception in 2007. With him is Flt Lt Albert Gregory, who illustrates the fact that not all of The Few were pilots. In the Battle Sgt Gregory was a Blenheim air gunner with No 219 Squadron. Both are wearing the tie of the BBFA. (Vic Seymour Photographic Services)

Battle of Britain Fighter Association – An organisation, founded in 1958, of which only holders of the Battle of Britain Clasp may be full members. At one time there were just over 1000 such members. The figure in the spring of 2009 was 104.

Battle of Britain Memorial Flight – The RAF's Historic Aircraft Flight was formed at Biggin Hill in 1957 and was

Two very different generations watch aircraft of the BBMF fly over the National Memorial at Capel-le-Ferne. On the right is Flt Lt Keith Lawrence, a New Zealander who fought in the Battle with No 234 and No 603 Squadrons and No 421 Flight. On November 26 he was shot down by Bf 109s over Ramsgate, his Spitfire disintegrating. He managed to open his parachute, landed in the sea with severe injuries and was picked up by a minesweeper. The decoration that Flt Lt Lawrence can be seen wearing on the extreme left is the DFC. Next to it is the 1939-45 Star with Battle of Britain Clasp. (Barry Duffield)

renamed the Battle of Britain Memorial Flight in 1973. In 2008 the Flight's aircraft strength was one Lancaster, five Spitfires, two Hurricanes, one Dakota and two Chipmunks. It was expected to make over 700 individual aircraft display appearances in that year.

Beaverbrook, Lord (1879-1964) – William Maxwell Aitken was born in Canada. While at school he had a newspaper round, wrote for a regional paper and founded a school newspaper. He intended to become a lawyer, but then went into business and became interested in politics.

Aitken visited Britain on a number of occasions and developed a friendship with the future Prime Minister, Andrew Bonar Law. In the General Election in December 1910, Aitken was elected as a Unionist MP for Ashton under Lyne, Lancashire. He was knighted in 1911 in recognition of his political financial contributions. His most famous involvement in newspaper publishing had already begun with an investment in the *Daily Express*.

He was heavily involved in politics during the First World War, serving as Minister of Information and joining the Cabinet as Chancellor of the Duchy of Lancaster. He became Lord Beaverbrook at this time, taking his title from a small community near where he had grown up in Canada.

Between the wars Beaverbrook developed his newspaper interests and moved in high political circles. He campaigned for Empire Free Trade, attacked Stanley Baldwin and argued that King Edward VIII should remain on the throne.

On May 14 1940 Churchill appointed Beaverbrook Minister of Aircraft Production and he joined the War Cabinet in August. He resigned as Minister in April 1941, but took further high Government appointments.

Beaverbrook's elder son, Sqn Ldr Max Aitken, was CO of No 601 Squadron at the start of the Battle of Britain, being posted away on July 20. Later in the war he commanded the Banff Mosquito Strike Wing and left the RAF as a Gp Capt. On the death of his father he disclaimed the peerage, but took the Baronetcy which Beaverbrook had also received.

Bentley Priory – The mansion at Stanmore, Middlesex which was the headquarters of Fighter Command during the Battle of Britain. The Priory was completed in 1766 and extensively changed from 1788 by Sir John Soane. Queen Adelaide, Queen Consort of William IV, died there in 1849. Later it was both a hotel and a school before the RAF arrived in the 1920s.

Air Chf Mshl Dowding used the library as his office when AO CinC Fighter Command and lived nearby in a house called "Montrose".

RAF occupation of Bentley Priory ceased early in 2008. Prior to this the Bentley Priory Battle of Britain Trust had been formed, on behalf of the Battle of Britain Fighter Association. Its objects were:-

Bentley Priory - headquarters of Fighter Command (Courtesy Bentley Priory Battle of Britain Trust)

"To establish and maintain Bentley Priory, Stanmore in the London Borough of Harrow as a centre for education, information, training and teaching of the history of the Battle of Britain, aerospace history, aerospace technology and its future advancement.

"To use Bentley Priory as a permanent memorial to those who served in the Royal Air Force and in particular (but not exclusively) during the Battle of Britain in order to assist future generations in acknowledging and recognising the sacrifices made during the Battle of Britain to ensure freedom of Europe and the World."

In July 2008, the London Borough of Harrow approved plans for the site, which would involve the creation of "exclusive" residences, as well as a museum ensuring the survival of the rooms most associated with the events of 1940.

Biggin Hill – Sector station C in No 11 Group, located between Bromley and Westerham in Kent. Built on land belonging to Earl Stanhope. The RFC began to use the airfield in 1917. At that time it was the Wireless Testing Park.

Biggin suffered major attacks during the Battle, including those of August 30, August 31 and September 1. On the 30th a shelter received a direct hit, causing many casualties. West Malling airfield was also in Sector C.

The station's nickname, "Biggin on the Bump" derives from two sources. The airfield stands out on a plateau when it is approached from the air and wartime pilots found that there was a runway bump.

In 1958 the RAF ceased flying from Biggin Hill and left altogether in 1992. Today the airfield is in civilian use as London Biggin Hill Airport. The St George's Royal Air Force Chapel of Remembrance is open almost every day and services are held on Saturdays and Sundays.

"The name has a homely sound, almost rustic, but there are squadrons of the Royal Air Force as proud of having fought from here as regiments in the Army are of having 'Blenheim'

A modern photograph of Dowding's office at Bentley Priory, preserved as it was in his day. (Courtesy RAF Museum)

Participants in a "battlefield tour" in 2008 pass E pens at East Camp, Biggin Hill. (Richard Hunting)

and 'Alamein' emblazoned on their colours." From *RAF Biggin Hill* by Graham Wallace.

Big Wing – Name applied to the theory that more damage could be inflicted on the enemy if they could be attacked by three or more squadrons acting together under one leader. The most visible proponents of the idea during the Battle were AVM Leigh-Mallory of No 12 Group and Sqn Ldr Douglas Bader, OC, No 242 Squadron within No 12 Group.

John Ray in *The Battle of Britain, New Perspectives*, argues that there was a second Big Wing controversy – a dispute on tactics between the Air Ministry and Fighter Command, which had its origins before the war. Bader became the point at which the two strands came together and found a champion who was charismatic, lacked fear, expressed his opinions forcibly and had the aura associated with having fought his way back to flying after grievous injuries.

The Big Wing, led by Bader, first saw action on September 7 when 22 victories were claimed.

Addressing this, Stephen Bungay in *The Most Dangerous Enemy* wrote, "From a comparison of actual German losses with pilots' combat reports it seems likely that the wing accounted for three Bf 110s and shared in the destruction of two others. They may also have got a couple of Bf 109s."

It is also the case that the appearance of such a force must have been a shock to the Luftwaffe at a time when Goering was persuading himself that Fighter Command was finished.

Here was epitomised the fundamental dispute between Park at No 11 Group and his opposite number at No 12 Group. Park (and many of his pilots) argued that a Big Wing took too long to form up and therefore missed opportunities to attack the bombers, particularly as they headed towards their targets. In any case, declared Park, with No 11 Group airfields the closest to France, it was not a tactic that was open to him.

Pilots in No 12 Group were wont to argue that the problem lay in the lateness of their calls to action.

The Big Wing also became known as the Duxford Wing. Some of its squadrons were based at the Cambridgeshire airfield (although No 242 Squadron was at Coltishall in Norfolk for much of the Battle) and Duxford was a rendezvous point.

See also entry on Dowding.

Black Thursday (Der Schwarze Donnerstag) – In the
Luftwaffe this denoted August 15, on which heavy casualties were suffered both in the south and during a raid launched on north east England from bases in Norway and Denmark.

The attack on the north east was instigated in the belief that the area had been denuded of fighters and anti-aircraft guns in support of the defence of southern England. For the largest German formation the first indication that this was not the case came at about 12.30 when, off the Farne Islands, it was attacked by 11 Spitfires of No 72 Squadron, which had been scrambled from Acklington.

On this day a Ju 87 crashed in Shornecliffe Crescent, More Hall, Folkestone, after hitting power lines, while being chased by RAF fighters. In 2008 the careful observer could still spot damage to property caused in the incident. The crew, Unteroffizier Herman Weber and Unteroffizier Franz Krauss were both killed.

Bogey – unidentified aircraft – probably hostile, but should be approached with care.

Bomber Command – Formed in 1936 to control home bomber forces and merged into Strike Command in 1968. During the Battle of Britain the Command operated Wellingtons, Whitleys, Blenheims, Hampdens and Battles against targets in Germany and the occupied countries, including ports where invasion barges were being assembled. Leaflet and mine laying ("Gardening") operations were also carried out.

In the Battle period the Command won two VCs. The first went to Flt Lt Roderick ("Babe") Learoyd, pilot of a No 49 Squadron Hampden, which, on the night of August 12/13, was part of a force tasked to attack an aqueduct carrying the Dortmund-Ems Canal over the River Ems, north of Munster. Learoyd and his crew were the fifth to approach the target and flew through blinding searchlights and intense flak and machine gun fire. Afterwards he nursed the badly damaged aircraft home and circled his base at Scampton to avoid a night landing. The attack was successful.

On the night of September 15/16, Sgt John Hannah was WOP/AG of a Hampden of No 83 Squadron, flown by Plt Off C A Connor, a Canadian, which attacked concentrations of invasion barges at Antwerp. The aircraft dropped its bombs, but was then hit by flak and set on fire. Two members of the crew baled out, but Hannah fought the fire until it was extinguished and then, despite severe burns, helped Connor to navigate the Hampden back to Scampton. Hannah received the VC and Connor the DFC.

Connor was lost in November, when his aircraft came down in the sea, having been hit by flak during an attack on Kiel. There were no survivors. Connor's crew on that occasion consisted of Sgt G H Stubbings, Sgt J W C Gibson and Sgt R Norris.

From the spring of 1940 Air Mshl Charles Portal was the AO CinC, Bomber Command. He became Sir Charles in July and left the post in early October, prior to succeeding Newall as CAS. He was replaced at Bomber Command by Air Mshl Sir Richard Peirse.

A number of Bomber Command pilots volunteered for Fighter Command and saw action during the Battle. One of them appears in the frequently published photograph of No 242 Squadron pilots on and in front of a Hurricane. Sadly, the presence of Fg Off Michael Homer means that the scene cannot have been captured in October or November as sometimes claimed. Homer, who had won the DFC as a

Pilots of No 242 Squadron. Standing second from the right is Fg Off Michael Homer, a volunteer from Bomber Command, who joined the Squadron on September 21 and was killed in action on September 27. He is buried in his home town of Swanage. (Courtesy of Imperial War Museum, London, negative no CH 1413)

Taken at Linton on Ouse in June, this photograph shows a No 58 Squadron Whitley crew preparing for action. (Courtesy of the Imperial War Museum, negative no CH 229.)

Hampden pilot with No 44 Squadron, joined 242 from No 1 Squadron on September 21 and was killed in action on September 27.

Boulton Paul Defiant – Monoplane fighter with gun turret mounted immediately behind the cockpit and Merlin engine, which made its first flight on August 11 1937. In the Battle it equipped No 141 and No 264 Squadrons.

During the Battle of France the Defiant enjoyed the element of surprise and a considerable number of German aircraft fell to its guns when mounting conventional attacks from the rear.

However, it did not take the Germans long to work out the limitations of the type including lack of speed and no forward firing armament. On May 13, over the Netherlands, five out of six Defiants of No 264 Squadron, operating from Martlesham Heath, were shot down by Bf 109s.

The brief participation of the two Defiant squadrons in the Battle of Britain produced a similar degree of loss and tragedy.

More success was achieved when the Defiant became a night fighter. Defiants were also used as target tugs and in an air/sea rescue role.

Bounce – (used as a verb) To inflict a surprise attack – often by Bf 109s. It has been suggested that it derives from a 1930s slang expression describing a man giving unwelcome attention to a lady, perhaps in the back of a taxi.

Defiants of No 264 Squadron at Kirton in Lindsey. (Courtesy of Imperial War Museum, London, negative no CH 880)

Brand, Air Vice Marshal Sir (Christopher Joseph) Quintin (1893-1968) – Born in South Africa and served in the South African Defence Force 1914/15, before joining the RFC, where he saw action on the Western Front and in the defence of south east England. On the night of May 19/20 1918, when CO of No 112 Squadron, he shot down a Gotha on the last German raid over England.

Brand reported that, "Soon after my opening fire the aircraft burst into flames, which also enveloped my own machine for an instant. The aircraft fell to earth in pieces over the south east side of the Isle of Sheppey."

For this action he was made DSO and he also received the MC and DFC for his services in the First World War.

In February/March 1920 Brand undertook a pioneering flight from England (Brooklands) to Cape Town in a Vickers Vimy, with another South African RFC veteran, Pierrie (later Pierre) van Ryneveld. Both were knighted. Brand later served at the Royal Aircraft Establishment, Farnborough and as Director General of Aviation in Egypt.

In July 1940 he took command of the newly formed No 10 Group, Fighter Command, covering the south west and south Wales. In this role he co-operated closely with Park at No 11 Group. Brand retired from the RAF in 1943.

Break – Injunction over the radio to take immediate evasive action – usually indicating that German fighters were behind the pilot or pilots addressed.

Inexperienced pilots were surprised at how, once they had obeyed, they could go in seconds from being part of a mass of aircraft to an empty sky. Sometimes, after that, the secondary main line of the Southern Railway, running across country from Tonbridge to Guildford could be a welcome navigational aid.

Bristol Beaufighter – A hastily conceived and developed aircraft based on the Bristol company's Beaufort and

Blenheim designs. The two-seater Beaufighter met a requirement for a well-armed night and long range escort fighter.

The first flight took place on July 17 1939. In September 1940 No 25 and No 29 Squadrons in Fighter Command began to receive Beaufighters and both were fully operational with the type the following month.

Some later aircraft carried torpedoes on anti-shipping strikes. Those serving with the RAAF against Japanese shipping gained the nickname, "Whispering Death". In later years the Beaufighter served the RAF as a target tug, the last example being withdrawn in 1960.

Bristol Blenheim – Aircraft with both fighter and bomber variants which was developed from a private project

Plt Off L G H Kells about to fly a night sortie in a Blenheim of No 29 Squadron. Kells was lost in 1941, failing to return from a Hurricane test flight. (Courtesy of Imperial War Museum, London, negative no CH 1584)

initiated by Lord Rothermere to produce aerial transport for his own use.

The Blenheim 1F was a development of the bomber version and fitted with an underbelly containing four .303in Browning machine guns, in addition to a Vickers machine gun in the dorsal (upper) turret. Power came from two Bristol Mercury air-cooled radial engines.

In the Battle nine squadrons and the FIU operated Blenheims, including No 236, No 238 and No 248 Squadrons, attached to Fighter Command from Coastal Command. The vulnerability of the type as a day fighter limited its role in the Battle. It also operated at night, but lacked the technology to achieve significant success.

Broadcast – A broadcast that made considerable impact at the time and that is still regularly referred to and quoted occurred on July 14. From the Kentish cliffs, BBC Air Correspondent, Charles Gardner watched and dramatically described aircraft fighting over a convoy in the Channel.

Gardner saw a burning aircraft falling, declaring, "there's somebody hit a German." He noted a descending parachute and then told his listeners, "he's a Junkers 87 and he's going slap into the sea."

Later evidence pointed to the aircraft Gardner observed being a Hurricane of No 615 Squadron, with Plt Off Michael Mudie the man who had baled out. He was rescued from the sea, badly wounded, by the Navy and died the next day.

Even without this knowledge, immediate reaction to Gardner's broadcast was mixed. He was both praised and accused of sounding as though he was commentating on a sporting contest. The debate has continued.

Gardner had been appointed the BBC's first air correspondent in 1937. Later in 1940 he joined the RAF, serving for a time as a pilot in Coastal Command. He resumed his post with the BBC after the war, before moving into the aircraft industry.

Towards the end of his BBC career Gardner's vivid turn of phrase received further worldwide attention. He persuaded the FAA to fly him from Culdrose, Cornwall, out into the Western Approaches to pass at 100 ft over the stricken American freighter, *Flying Enterprise*. Still on board the ship were its skipper, Kurt Carlsen and Kenneth Dancy, mate of the Admiralty tug, *Turmoil*. Both men were rescued before the ship sank.

Charles Gardner died in 1983.

Many journalists used the cliffs between Folkestone and Dover as a vantage point, particularly during the early part of the Battle of Britain. A camp of photographers was established.

Buster – Order to use full throttle, normally to reach an enemy formation as quickly as possible.

Call signs – Squadrons and those they were communicating with while airborne used call signs for identity purposes. Examples of squadron call signs were Jacko (No 32 Squadron), Baffin (No 56), Kotel (No 222) and Dogrose (No 610). No 1 Squadron (RCAF) used, appropriately, Caribou, a North American name for reindeer.

Camm Sydney (1893-1966) – Secretary of the Windsor Model Aeroplane Club at 19. During his stewardship the club built a glider and a project to produce a powered aircraft was halted by the outbreak of the First World War. Camm then joined the Martinsyde aeroplane company at Brooklands. In 1923, after the demise of Martinsyde, he became senior draughtsman at Hawker, rising to Chief Designer in two years.

The Hawker Hart light bomber was an early Camm design, appearing in 1928. This was developed into the Fury fighter.

In 1934 the Air Ministry issued a specification for a monoplane eight-gun fighter and Camm's response was the Hurricane. Later designs for which he was responsible included the Typhoon, which entered RAF service in 1941 and, in the jet age, the Hunter.

Camm was knighted in 1953.

"As an aircraft designer Camm was pre-eminent during the exciting early years of aviation." Oxford Dictionary of National Biography

Casualties – During the Battle, 544 of the men who qualified for the 1939-45 Star with Battle of Britain clasp, died from all causes or were mortally wounded and died later.

"There was hardly anybody left of the pilots who started out with me. All one's friends had gone." AVM "Birdie" Bird-Wilson looking back on the Battle.

Then let us remember and while there's an ember

Of love for those young hearts at rest in the grave

To show by each deed the land that they freed

Is worthy of all that those dear lads gave

Last verse of poem signed "RJC" which appeared in the magazine of Salesian College, Farnborough, Hampshire after the deaths on successive days in the Battle of the brothers Fg Off Patrick Woods-Scawen (No 85 Squadron) and Plt Off Anthony Woods-Scawen (No 43 Squadron). Both were old boys of the school.

Dear Mrs Case

I have hesitated long before writing to send you some first hand news of your boy's heroic end, and a piece of the Spitfire which I thought you might like to have.

I was staying at Capel-le-Ferne when the plane came down, two fields away from the bungalow, my husband and his platoon were on the spot instantly and his boys 70th Buffs had to do the guarding.

We had been watching the fight when nine Messerschmitts swooped into two of ours. Everyone was terribly upset when the Spitfire was shot down. I have seldom seen my husband so affected, but he assured me that the boy must have been killed in the air before he crashed. I thought this knowledge might be of some small comfort to you in your tragic sorrow, and pride in the astonishing courage of these sons whose deeds fill the world with admiration.

Forgive me for intruding, this is not meant like that, and requires no answer.

Plt Off Herbert Case on leave with his family in Somerset shortly before he was shot down and killed. His friend, Plt Off Hugh Reilley of No 66 Squadron, also killed shortly afterwards, joined him on that leave. (Case family)

The text of a letter sent by an Army officer's wife to the mother of Plt Off Herbert Case of No 72 Squadron, lost in action on October 12. While it may be true that Plt Off Case was killed in the air, such accounts often contained this suggestion, as a means of providing comfort.

Herbert Case's body was placed on a gate, used as a makeshift stretcher and taken to the edge of the field in which he crashed, to await collection by the RAF. In recent years a battered RAF button has been found at that spot, which may well have come from his uniform.

Churchill, Winston Leonard Spencer (1874-1965) –

With a long career as a soldier, statesman, journalist and novelist already to his credit, Churchill's final ascent to the pinnacle of history began with the outbreak of the Second World War. The Prime Minister, Neville Chamberlain, made him First Lord of the Admiralty, with a place in the War Cabinet. Legend has it that the Admiralty signalled the Fleet, "Winston is back" (he had held the same post in the previous great conflict), but the evidence for this seems scant.

Churchill played a leading role in the conduct of the campaign in Norway, after Germany had invaded that country and Denmark on April 9. The campaign was a failure and Churchill found himself defending the Government's position in the House of Commons on May 8 during a two-day debate.

A crucial moment in the debate came when the Conservative MP Leo Amery addressed the Government, quoting Cromwell's injunction to the Long Parliament.

"You have sat too long here for any good you have been doing. Depart I say and let us have done with you. In the name of God go."

According to Amery's own account, although he had brought the words with him, it was only at the last moment, judging the mood of the House, that he decided to use them.

The vote at the end of the debate resulted in a Government majority of 81 – in theory it could have been 213. About 100 Government supporters voted with the Labour Party or abstained, though Churchill was with the majority.

The Prime Minister and Mrs Churchill on their way to visit the London docks, September 25 1940. (Courtesy Imperial War Museum, London, negative no H 4367)

This led to the formation of a coalition government. The Labour Party would not serve under Chamberlain. On May 10 Churchill held off the threat of Lord Halifax to become Prime Minister. Halifax had little inclination for putting himself forward, partly because of his lack of military understanding. History also remembers this day as the start of the German Blitzkrieg.

Between then and the Battle of Britain Churchill strove to keep France in the war and Italy out of it. During June he met with defeats on both counts, but was more successful, at a micro level, in gaining control of his war cabinet. It is often forgotten now that this is one of the battles he had to fight, overcoming, with Chamberlain's help, the view that a negotiated peace with Germany was an option.

In July he was in a position, as Roy Jenkins his 2001 biographer pointed out, to apply himself to some less weighty matters. For instance, he resisted the wish of the Duke of Windsor (formerly King Edward VIII) to return to England from Portugal. Churchill ensured that he became Governor of the Bahamas. The Prime Minister declined to release soldiers to act as servants to the Duke and then warned him about expressing a view on the Germans or Hitler, "which is different from that adopted by the British nation and Parliament."

One of Churchill's most remembered public appearances of the Battle occurred on Sunday September 8. In the hours after the East End of London had suffered terribly for the first time at the hands of the Luftwaffe, he appeared in the area amongst the rubble. A week later he visited the No 11 Group HQ at Uxbridge, on what became known as Battle of Britain Day.

On this occasion a famous exchange occurred.

"What other reserves have we?" Churchill asked AVM Park.

"There are none," was the reply.

Another Prime Ministerial excursion was on October 7 when he went with Lieutenant General Pile to see AA guns in Richmond Park and balloons in Kent.

Churchill would remain Prime Minister until the evening of July 26 1945, when, defeated in a long drawn out General Election, he went to Buckingham Palace to resign. He would lead the country again from 1951 to 1955, with his health and vigour in steady decline. He died on January 24 1965.

Winston Churchill's many honours included being sworn of the Privy Council in 1907, made a Companion of Honour in 1922 and receiving the Order of the Garter in 1953. He declined a Dukedom, but received the Nobel Prize for Literature in 1953 and was made an honorary citizen of the United States in 1963. Further honour across the Atlantic came posthumously in 1999 when a guided missile destroyer was named USS *Winston S Churchill*.

A number of "The Few" walked in Churchill's funeral cortege. They were, "Ricky" Wright, Pete Brothers, Leonard Bartlett, Dickie Haine, "Ras" Berry, "Bertie" Wootten, John Ellacombe, Al Deere, Geoffrey Brunner, Roy Dutton, Alec Ingle, Desmond Sheen, Bobby Oxspring and George Westlake.

Circle of Death – Defensive formation adopted by Bf 110s under attack.

Civilian services – Many civilian organisations including police forces, fire and ambulance services, ARP, Salvation Army, WVS and RNLI played their parts in the Battle, as did individual civilians.

Firemen had sometimes been viewed as "war dodgers" during the Phoney War. However, from September 1940 the men and women of the fire services were in the front line, great heroism was shown and many lives were lost.

Just after midnight on September 7/8, hours after the first mass raid on London had begun, the LFB recorded nine conflagrations (fires requiring over 100 pumps and out of control), 19 major (at least 30 pumps) fires, 40 serious (10 or more pumps) fires and 1,000 lesser fires.

A railway arch in south-east London is utilised as a shelter. (Courtesy Imperial War Museum, London, negative number D 1605)

"Five hundred pumps ordered to West Ham alone .... sped eastwards to attend fires in ships' warehouses ... 250 acres of tall timber stacks blazed out of control in the Surrey Commercial Docks, the rum quay buildings in the West India Docks, alight from end to end, molten pitch from a stricken tar distillery flooded the road, bringing to a halt all emergency vehicles ... it was a scene of horror and chaos as Civil Defence workers, themselves shocked and terrified by their first experience of the Blitz, dug into the debris of demolished buildings in search of casualties ." So wrote Cyril Demarne in *The London Blitz – A Fireman's Tale.*

The ARP Act of 1937 had made it compulsory for local authorities to take appropriate measures to prepare for air raids. As with the fire service, men serving in ARP roles were particularly liable to abuse during the Phoney War.

Fire fighters in action, Oxford Street, London, September 18 (Roy Goodey collection)

Gradually the term "Civil Defence" came to be used in preference to ARP and both were part of popular parlance during the Battle.

When the bombing came, the duties of ARP wardens included reporting the fall of bombs, fires, presence of gas, blocked roads, damaged drains, etc to their ARP control centre. They also guided and helped the public, allaying panic, directing those in the street to the nearest shelter when a raid was imminent.

Gas, electricity and GPO engineers were unsung heroes in helping to restore the operational capability of airfields after bomb damage – often working in dangerous, or at least highly unpleasant, conditions.

The first civilian death from enemy action in Britain occurred at Bridge of Waithe, Orkney on March 16 1940. During an enemy attack on Scapa and Kirkwall a bomb struck the house of Miss Isabella Macleod. From his home across the road, 27-year-old James Ibister, married with a baby son, went to help. He was caught in the blast of a second bomb and killed. Miss Macleod was injured but survived.

The last civilian death resulting from enemy action was that of Mrs Ivy Millichamp, aged 34, who was killed in her kitchen in Kynaston Road, Orpington, Kent, by the last rocket of the war on March 27 1945. Her husband Eric, in another part of the house, was injured.

Clasp – Aircrew who flew operationally with Fighter Command in the Battle became entitled to the "immediate" award of the 1939-45 Star, with a Battle of Britain clasp, the only clasp issued with the Star.

The discussion on how "The Few" should be recognised and which men should be entitled to an award was going on soon after the Battle and continued for many years. Indeed, the discussion on participants continues in a lower key today.

An important moment came in 1944. In a debate in the House of Commons, on war decorations and medals, Sir Ronald Ross Bt (Unionist, Londonderry) argued for recognition for the fighter pilots of the Battle of Britain. He proposed an emblem to be worn on the 1939-45 Star and received support from other MPs and, in correspondence, from the Air Minister.

In May 1945 the announcement was made of a clasp to the Star for aircrew of Fighter Command operational between July 1 and October 31 1940. The start date was amended to July 10 (the date chosen by Dowding in his 1941 report) in June 1946.

An order in July 1945 (which used July 10 as the start of the Battle) gave a list of squadrons whose personnel qualified. Additions to, and deletions from this, were made for 16 years, until the list of 71 squadrons and units recognised today was established.

The July 1945 order stated, "COs are not to admit claims for this highly-prized emblem which are open to any possible doubt. The clasp is not available for personnel who flew in aircraft other than fighters, notwithstanding that they may have been engaged with the enemy in the air during the qualifying period."

In 1942 Captain Bruce Ingram, owner of the *Illustrated London News*, had written to the Air Minister, comparing the Battle with the defeat of the Spanish Armada and the victory of Trafalgar and proposing a permanent record of those who had "played an active part" in the Battle of Britain. The immediate official attitude was that the list should be limited to those killed in the Battle. Eventually, a roll of honour was prepared and presented to Westminster Abbey which included the names of all RAF aircrew killed in the July 10-October 31 period.

Further progress in establishing a master list of names of participants was made from 1955, when Flt Lt John Holloway, who had been ground crew with No 615 Squadron in the Battle, obtained signatures of members of The Few while scenes for the film *Reach for the Sky* were being shot at Kenley. He eventually determined to attempt to collect the signatures of all participants in the Battle, but needed to establish the names of those whose signatures he should be collecting.

Extensive research followed. Holloway became the acknowledged expert on the subject and, in 1961, his list of 2,937 names was published in *The Narrow Margin* by Derek Wood and Derek Dempster. In 1969 Holloway presented to the IWM his collection of 2,200 signatures, including many of those who had died in the Battle, leaders such as Churchill and engineers such as Mitchell and Camm.

From its formation in 1958 the BBFA naturally took an interest in who was entitled to membership and carried out much work, in consultation with Holloway and through successive archivists (and Battle veterans) Gp Capt Tom Gleave and Wg Cdr John Young. Their work, together with that of the AHB and other researchers, building on Holloway's efforts, led to more public recognition of the individual members of The Few in the lists displayed on the Christopher Foxley-Norris Memorial Wall at Capel-le-Ferne and the Monument on London's embankment, both unveiled in 2005.

Mrs Mimi Thompson at the Christopher Foxley-Norris Memorial Wall at Capel-le-Ferne on which all The Few are listed. Mrs Thompson is the widow of Gp Capt Peter Thompson who, in 1940, was a Plt Off flying Hurricanes with No 32 and No 605 Squadrons. (Vic Seymour Photographic Services)

There seems little doubt that minor changes to the list will be made from time to time.

"...Gieves [the tailor] has issued a tie to Sqn Ldr R Carnall, who says he was a Sergeant Pilot in 111 Squadron from February 1937 to August 1940. Is he OK?" Extract from a letter dated August 6 1959 written by Wg Cdr Bobby Oxspring, on behalf of the BBFA, to Flt Lt Holloway, raising a number of similar queries. Sqn Ldr Carnall's credentials as one of The Few were impeccable.

Commanding Officers – A fighter squadron in the Battle was normally led by a Squadron Leader, with Flight Lieutenants commanding A Flight and B Flight.

Some achieved relative longevity. Examples of COs who commanded squadrons throughout the Battle were Sqn Ldr George Denholm of No 603 and Sqn Ldr Harry Hogan of No 501. Both survived the war and died in old age.

In contrast was the experience of No 253 Squadron. Sqn Ldr Harold Starr was machine-gunned and killed under his parachute by a Bf 109 at about 8.25am on August 31. The former CO, Sqn Ldr Tom Gleave, still flying with the squadron as a supernumerary, assumed command, only to be shot down and grievously burned over Biggin Hill three and a half hours later. Flt Lt Bill Cambridge, the senior flight commander, assumed command. Sqn Ldr Gerry Edge took over on September 5 and Flt Lt Cambridge was killed the next day.

Some COs believed that the job was essentially one of ensuring that the squadron was combat ready and leading the squadron in action, while others paid more attention to administration and flew less often.

The casualty rate meant that some officers became COs despite little or no recent relevant experience. The New Zealander, Sqn Ldr Terence Lovell-Gregg, was in this category when he took command of No 87 Squadron on July

Sqn Ldr Donald MacDonell, CO of No 64 Squadron, leaves his Spitfire, while behind, the ground crew are at work. Perhaps it is not fanciful to detect the physical and mental strain of leadership in 1940 on Sqn Ldr MacDonell's face. He became a PoW in 1941, survived the war and retired from the RAF as an Air Cdre. He was one of the pilots drawn by Cuthbert Orde. (Courtesy British Movietone News)

Sqn Ldr Philip Hunter (extreme left) of No 264 Squadron holds a briefing. He and his gunner, Fred King had achieved much success during the Battle of France. Hunter was awarded the DSO and King received the DFM and was commissioned from LAC. They failed to return on August 24, having been last seen chasing Ju 88s following an attack on Manston. Both are remembered at Runnymede. (Courtesy of Imperial War Museum, London, negative no CH 196)

12 and was respected for being prepared to fly behind the flight commanders while he gained experience. He was lost on August 15, leading five Hurricanes into at least 120 German aircraft over Lyme Bay.

Sqn Ldr "Jimmy" Fenton, a former army co-operation pilot and instructor, took over No 238 Squadron on July 15 and led it for the rest of the Battle, although he was away wounded for over a month. He later rose to the rank of Air Cdre and had a highly successful post war business career. At the end of his life in the 1990s he was still corresponding with the survivors of 238, was still able to name all those who had died under his command and was still concerned that, with more experience, he could have done more to save them.

One of the "inexperienced" COs (Sqn Ldr Hill Harkness of No 257 Squadron) was removed for his lack of enthusiasm

for confronting the enemy. He left a squadron which had suffered heavy casualties and where morale was extremely low.

Controllers – Group controllers, or sometimes AOCs, took decisions on which squadrons should be deployed and when. It was generally Sector controllers who then directed the interception of enemy formations, seeking to place the squadrons in the best possible position for a successful attack.

The quality of the communication with airborne squadrons seems to have varied. The senior No 11 Group controller, Wg Cdr Lord Willoughby de Broke impressed with his calm and clear messages.

On the other hand, Flt Lt "Sammy" Hall recalled the occasion when No 152 Squadron was flying from Warmwell to make an interception, urged on by an over enthusiastic controller. Eventually the man on the ground was temporarily silenced when an unidentified pilot told him to, "Get off the bloody air", adding that he was a "stupid clot".

On September 7 AVM Park issued an instruction drawing attention to the number of squadrons failing to intercept incoming raids. He pointed out that controllers were sending aircraft in too high and squadrons were adding height to the instructions they were given.

A task for controllers after a period of fighting was over was to direct airborne squadrons to the best available airfield, if bomb damage meant that they could not return to their own.

That the word of the controller was not always law was illustrated to the pilots of No 610 Squadron at the end of August. In the process of moving north from Biggin Hill to Acklington for a rest the squadron spent a night at Kirton in Lindsey. As the Spitfires lifted off the following morning the controller requested that they search for a reported hostile. To the relief of his weary men, the response from Sqn Ldr John Ellis was a curt refusal.

Convoy CW9 (or Peewit) Battle of – This westbound convoy (CW9 to the Navy, Peewit to the RAF) consisted of 20 merchant ships, whose principal cargo was coal, and a naval escort. It sailed from the Thames Estuary on the night of August 7 and the next day came under constant German attack, first by E Boats and later by the Luftwaffe, with enormous aerial fights developing, particularly off the Isle of Wight.

RAF squadrons involved included No 43, No 145, No 238 and No 257 (Hurricanes) and No 609 (Spitfires).

Only four merchant ships reached Swanage unscathed and there were heavy aircraft and aircrew casualties on both sides, but the RAF was widely considered to have come out on top.

Especial praise seems to have been given to No 145 Squadron, led by Sqn Ldr John Peel, which had been engaged over Peewit three times, had claimed 21 German aircraft destroyed and lost five pilots killed.

Amongst the congratulations received by the squadron at Westhampnett, was a message from Air Chf Mshl Newall, CAS, which read, "Well done 145 Squadron in your hard fighting today. Good work by all."

Four days after the action the PM ordered that a telegram be sent to Air Chf Mshl Dowding, stating, "The War Cabinet would be glad if you would convey to the fighter squadrons of the RAF, engaged in Thursday's brilliant action their admiration of the skill and prowess which they displayed and congratulate them on the defeat and heavy losses inflicted on a far more numerous enemy."

Crash sites – In the circumstances of 1940, examination of places where aircraft crashed was often perfunctory. On many occasions since the war aviation archaeologists have excavated the sites of crashes from the Battle. Their activities have led to the discovery of remains and artefacts and to some controversy. Such activities are now strictly controlled by the MoD.

On occasions a result of excavation has been the need for a second funeral.

A case in point was the Hurricane flown by Sgt Dennis Noble of No 43 Squadron which crashed into Woodhouse Road, Hove, Sussex at about 11.50am on August 30, having been shot down by a Bf 109. A funeral for Sgt Noble took place at East Retford cemetery, Nottinghamshire, near his home.

Generally at the time a coroner required the discovery of 7lb of remains and evidence of vital body parts, as well as proof of identity, to allow the death of a specific individual to be recorded.

In 1996 a further excavation was authorised and was carried out by the Southern Counties Aviation Club. Much of the skeleton of Sgt Noble was discovered. Artefacts uncovered included his parachute, cap, wallet, address book and prayer book.

Another funeral was held at East Retford in 1997.

Debden – Sector station F in No 11 Group, built as a fighter airfield during the RAF expansion period and operational from 1937, initially with three Gladiator squadrons. On April 25 1975, a Hurricane and Spitfire flypast marked closure. Today the Army's Carver Barracks occupies part of the site.

Castle Camps airfield was also in the Sector.

Decorations – Apart from the VC (see separate entry), the decorations normally awarded to RAF aircrew for gallantry in action in 1940 were the Distinguished Service Order (DSO), the Distinguished Flying Cross (DFC) and the Distinguished Flying Medal (DFM).

The DSO had been instituted in 1886 for officers and involved admission to an order; until the early years of the First World War some awards were made for services not performed under fire. At its institution it was available to both the Royal Navy and Army – in due course the RAF was added. As a gallantry decoration, the DSO ranked immediately below the VC.

The DFC was instituted by a Royal Warrant of June 3 1918, just over two months after the formation of the RAF. This warrant also established the DFM and the Air Force Cross (AFC) and Air Force Medal (AFM). The AFC and the AFM were awarded for courage or devotion to duty while flying, but not during operations against the enemy.

The DFC was awarded to officers and warrant officers and the DFM to other ranks for an act or acts of valour, courage or devotion to duty performed "whilst flying in active operations against the enemy". The awards were equivalent to the Royal Navy's Distinguished Service Cross (DSC) and Distinguished Service Medal (DSM) and the Army's Military Cross (MC) and Military Medal (MM).

Following a fundamental review of the system for gallantry awards, instigated by the then Prime Minister, John Major, in 1993, the DFM and the other service equivalents ceased to be awarded and all ranks became eligible for those previously awarded only to officers and warrant officers.

The DFCs awarded to the brothers Fg Off Patrick Woods-Scawen and Plt Off Anthony Woods-Scawen. Patrick was known as "Weasel" or "Woody" on No 85 Squadron and Anthony was "Wombat" on No 43 Squadron. (Woods-Scawen family)

In 1940 there was no decoration for RAF other ranks at the second level, that is between the VC and the DFM, although the Royal Navy had the Conspicuous Gallantry Medal (CGM) and the Army the Distinguished Conduct Medal (DCM). On November 10 1942 the CGM became available to other ranks of the Army and the RAF for deeds, "whilst flying in active operations against the enemy".

In the 1993 changes the second level awards of all three services were replaced by the Conspicuous Gallantry Cross (CGC), with the DSO reserved for outstanding leadership and service on military operations.

Some RAF and WAAF personnel who performed gallant acts, not in the air, during the Battle of Britain received Royal Navy and Army awards.

Dispersals – Points around an airfield at which aircraft were kept to reduce their vulnerability as targets. At East Camp, Biggin Hill in 2008, survivals included a dispersal hut, E (or blast) pens and shelters.

Aircraft were also dispersed to satellite airfields, which often had primitive facilities, far removed from the standards of pre-war RAF messes.

Dogfight – Expression indicating a melee of fighter aircraft in combat. For a number of reasons (including the relatively small amounts of fuel and ammunition carried by fighters on both sides) dogfights were rarer in the Battle than is generally supposed.

Onlookers were reminded of fighting dogs.

Dogs – Plenty of squadrons had one or more dogs, which often appeared in photographs. On No 152 Squadron, for instance, "Pilot Officer Pooch" was officially on the strength, though he seems to have belonged to Fg Off "Cocky" Cox.

Living in different circumstances was the mongrel known as Rip, which, in 1940, attached himself to a London ARP

warden and found many people trapped by bombing. In 1945 he received the PDSA Dickin Medal and was buried in 1946 at Ilford, Essex. The headstone records that, "he played his part in the Battle of Britain".

Dowding, Air Chief Marshal Sir Hugh Caswall Tremenheere (1882-1970) – Born at Moffat, Dumfriesshire, of Wiltshire ancestry. Educated at St Ninian's Preparatory School in Moffat (where his father was Headmaster) and at Winchester College. Entered the RMA, Woolwich in 1899 and commissioned into Royal Garrison Artillery, 1900. He went on to serve in Gibraltar, Ceylon, Hong Kong and India.

He acquired the nickname "Stuffy" which applied to the demeanour he normally adopted on duty. However, according to Vincent Orange, his most recent biographer,

Dowding was "the soul of formal courtesy" when dealing with subordinates and men and women who worked as hard as he did. He was a good listener and backed those who made a case. Early on he acquired the reputation of being a maverick, which would stay with him.

Orange says that Dowding could be "jovial" with polo or skiing companions and with his immediate family.

Dowding's career moved forward, with acceptance at the Staff College, Camberley in 1912. In the following year he became a Captain and qualified as a pilot, having paid for his own tuition. After a period at the CFS and a return to the Artillery, Dowding joined the RFC on the outbreak of war, later going across the Channel, initially as an observer with No 6 Squadron. He reverted to pilot status and then became a staff officer, before returning to England and the command of an experimental wireless unit at Brooklands in Surrey. Later in the war he commanded No 16 Squadron and No 9 Wing, both in France.

In these years Trenchard was in some respects unimpressed by Dowding and the latter disagreed with his superior's emphasis on offensive action.

Nonetheless, Dowding received a permanent commission as a Gp Capt and commanded No 1 Group at Kenley, before staff appointments, including a spell in Iraq. As Director of Training at the Air Ministry he earned more respect from Trenchard. He went back to the Middle East and wrote reports on the security situation there which added further to his reputation.

AVM Dowding joined the Air Council in 1930 as Air Member for Supply and Research. Shortly afterwards he sanctioned the air worthiness certificate of the airship R101.

During 1933 he became an Air Mshl and was made a KCB. From 1935 he held the title, Air Member for Research and Development.

In July 1936 Dowding was appointed to lead the newly created Fighter Command. Promotion to Air Chf Mshl followed in January 1937. Under his command the defensive system initiated in the First World War and developed since that time, grew to the point where it was able to play a decisive part in the fighting of 1940. He pressed for the building of all-weather runways and ensured the building of such features of Battle of Britain airfields as blast pens and air raid shelters.

Dowding also battled with various conflicting interests, including the powerful "bombers are more important" lobby, to obtain the aircraft he wanted, particularly Spitfires and Hurricanes. Further, he struggled to ensure that these aircraft were properly equipped. One argument he won was over the provision of bullet proof windscreens. Dowding had argued that if Chicago gangsters could have such glass for their cars, then the airmen of Fighter Command should have it for their aircraft.

In 1939 Dowding's three-year term at Fighter Command was due to expire and it was planned that his replacement would be Air Mshl Sir Christopher Courtney. Partly through the fact that Courtney was injured in an air crash, this never took place. Various dates were set for Dowding's departure and then extensions given.

Convinced that successful home defence demanded a strong Fighter Command (and a strong Navy) Dowding was greatly concerned, with the advent of war, by the despatch of Hurricanes to assist the French.

Matters reached a crisis in mid May. Famously Dowding wrote to the War Cabinet on May 16, including the words, "If the Home Defence force is drained away in desperate attempts to remedy the situation in France, defeat in France will involve the final, complete and irremediable defeat of this country."

When the Battle of Britain came, Dowding, his commanders and the organisation he had developed and fought for obsessively, ensured that air superiority over southern England was maintained. Thus there could be no German invasion. German incompetence played its part, but the argument has often been put that, but for Dowding and his victory, later land, sea and air victories would not have been possible.

In the early part of the Battle Dowding's son, Plt Off Derek Dowding, flew as a Spitfire pilot in No 74 Squadron.

Possibly the manner of Dowding's removal, with hindsight almost in the hour of his triumph and the failure to find a further suitable role for him, are more perplexing than the fact that he left Fighter Command.

There was intrigue against him, when he was at Bentley Priory and later. The best known manifestation of this was the Big Wing theory propounded in No 12 Group, which involved three, or even more, fighter squadrons forming up and attacking the enemy together.

On October 17, a meeting to discuss fighter tactics and developments in night interception was chaired by AVM Sholto Douglas, Deputy CAS. AVM Leigh-Mallory of No 12 Group astonished Dowding by attending with Sqn Ldr Douglas Bader, CO of No 242 Squadron. Bader was not only an arch and articulate proponent of "Big Wing", but, as Dowding noted, considerably more junior than anyone else at the discussion. However, neither Dowding nor Park objected to Bader's presence.

At this point the tide was clearly running in favour of Leigh-Mallory and against Dowding and Park. Bader's views received much attention from others present. Vincent Orange refers to the (unsurprising) "careworn appearance" of Dowding and Park on this occasion, compared with others present.

Here perhaps is an indication of Dowding's key weakness. He had long doubted Leigh-Mallory's ability as a fighter leader, yet the AOC, No 12 Group was still in place. At the same time Dowding had failed to ensure that Park and Leigh-Mallory, his two key subordinates, were obeying his orders and working together. At a time of scheming and plotting Dowding's personality and the attributes that had enabled him to achieve victory, put him at a disadvantage.

Many feel that it was to his great credit that scheming in the corridors of power was not something at which he was competent.

Arguments deployed in the debate over Dowding's future at this point also included, his age, seniority, length of time in post, the strain he had been under and (perhaps most importantly) the pressing need to find a means of destroying enemy aircraft at night.

Now that 70 years have passed most of these arguments seem far less substantial than they may have done at the time. Nevertheless they represent views that were sincerely held in some quarters in 1940.

It must also be remembered that in the late autumn of 1940 few if any people in Britain realised the extent of the victory that had been achieved.

Dowding himself acknowledged that point in the preface he wrote to Basil Collier's book, *Leader of The Few*, published in 1957.

So Dowding was told that he would go by Sinclair, Secretary of State for Air, in a meeting on November 13 and left Fighter Command on November 25. He was replaced by Sholto Douglas.

Dowding's further service hardly befitted his talents. He led an aircraft purchasing mission to the United States and subsequently headed a project to find ways of achieving economies in the RAF. Official retirement took place on July 14 1942.

Honours did come to Dowding. Before the Battle had ended he had been made GCB. In June 1943 he became Lord Dowding of Bentley Priory.

Efforts to gain him promotion to MRAF were fruitless, despite an intervention by the King. The feeling that this failure was an insult to Dowding has grown over the years.

When Dowding died in 1970 his ashes were buried in the RAF Chapel in Westminster Abbey.

King George VI and Queen Elizabeth, escorted by Air Chf Mshl Dowding, at Bentley Priory, September 1940. (Courtesy of Imperial War Museum, London, negative no CH 1233)

In 1988, HM Queen Elizabeth the Queen Mother unveiled a statue of Dowding outside the RAF Church of St Clement Danes in The Strand in Central London.

"Stuffy Dowding was a great commander and to this day we, his pilots, remember him with respect and affection and think he should have been made an MRAF." Wg Cdr John Beazley writing in 2003.

"The only commander who won one of the few decisive battles in history and got sacked for his pains." MRAF Sir Arthur Harris.

"One of those great men whom this country miraculously produces in times of peril." Denis Healey, Secretary of State for Defence, speaking at the interment of Lord Dowding's ashes in Westminster Abbey.

Dowding System – Name used for the system of British defences in 1940, in the air and on the ground. These had been largely developed since Fighter Command had been formed with Dowding in command. Others, of course, made major contributions to the system's development and success.

Chain Home stations detected German raids as they formed up and information was transmitted to the filter room at Bentley Priory where a picture of the situation was built up and allocated a number to each incoming raid. Information then went to the Bentley Priory operations room and onwards from there to Groups, Sectors and the Observer Corps. The latter watched and reported as raids crossed the coast and travelled inland, where radar could not follow them. Groups would order Sectors to scramble squadrons.

Other defences including Anti-Aircraft Command and Balloon Commands were co-ordinated by Fighter Command as part of the defence effort.

The Germans at the time did not fully understand how the British system worked.

Duxford – Sector station G in No 12 Group. Duxford and its satellite Fowlmere, were developed in 1917/18 for the RFC/RAF. Fowlmere closed in the 1920s and later re-opened.

Today IWM Duxford has become a magnet for aviation enthusiasts.

Duxford Wing – See entry for Big Wing.

Elham – Village (pronounced Eel-um) behind Folkestone, Kent which, because of its position, witnessed a considerable number of incidents during 1940 and which was the home of a dump for crashed Luftwaffe aircraft.

On July 8 the first German fighter to come down in Britain forced-landed nearby on Bladbean Hill. The pilot of the Bf 109, Leutnant Johann Boem, was taken prisoner. He had been shot down by a Spitfire flown by Sgt Edward Mould of No 74 Squadron.

An example from the Battle itself was the descent by parachute on August 29 of another 109 pilot, Oberleutnant Eckhart Priebe, who astonished villagers with his command of English.

Priebe's aircraft fell in Elham Park Wood and, on September 5, a Spitfire also crashed into the wood. Two brothers, Walter and William Wood, who were working nearby, tried to reach the pilot in the blazing wreckage but were unsuccessful. Later the remains of Sgt Malcolm "Mabel" Gray of No 72 Squadron were recovered.

Evill, AVM Douglas Claude Stathern (1892-1971) – Born at Broken Hill, New South Wales, Australia, Evill was educated in England and became a cadet at the Royal Naval College, first at Osborne and then at Dartmouth. He was commissioned in 1913 and learned to fly in the same year.

Evill spent much of the First World War flying in France with the RNAS and earned the DSC, as well as the AFC after receiving a permanent commission in the RAF. In the interwar period he commanded flying boat bases and No 70 Squadron in Iraq, held appointments at the RAF College, Cranwell and the RAF Staff College and was Deputy Director of War Organization at the Air Ministry.

In 1936, as an Air Cdre, he became SASO, Bomber Command and then, with promotion to AVM, he took charge of the Command's administration. He was part of an RAF mission in 1937 to inspect the new Luftwaffe. Early in the Second World War he was SASO of the British air forces in France, before becoming SASO at Fighter Command, playing a significant role, from his desk at Bentley Priory, in controlling the Command in the Battle of Britain and the Blitz. He sought to shield Dowding from much detail and interference and was highly critical of the treatment his boss received.

Dowding said of "Strath" Evill, "I could not have had a sounder or more reliable man supporting me during that time. He was always there, always on the job and always so pleasant in that quiet way of his."

Respectful comment was made on Evill's demeanour when he lost one of his sons. On the night of August 18/19 1941, Plt Off William Evill, aged 18, was the pilot of a No 10 Squadron Whitley from Leeming, tasked to attack Cologne. The aircraft came down in Belgium and there were no survivors.

Promoted to Air Mshl in 1942, Evill led the RAF delegation in Washington and became Vice CAS.

Air Chf Mshl Sir Douglas Evill retired from the RAF in 1947. He was then Director General of the English Speaking Union until 1949.

Douglas Evill – Dowding's 'reliable man'. (Courtesy of the Imperial War Museum, London, negative no CH 16275)

ff

Fairey Fulmar – Fleet Air Arm two-seat fighter, manufactured at Heaton Chapel, Stockport, which first flew at Ringway (now Manchester Airport) on January 4 1940. Fulmars equipped 808 Squadron, FAA in the Battle, when the second crew member was dispensed with. In ornithology there are two species of Fulmar in the petrel family.

Fighter Command – At the time of the RAF expansion plan of 1935, five Home Commands were created to replace Air Defence of Great Britain which had been established in 1925. These were Bomber, Coastal, Training, Maintenance and Fighter Commands. The latter came into being on July 14 1936, with Air Mshl Sir Hugh Dowding as AO CinC. In 1968 Fighter Command became part of the new Strike Command. For a short period in the Second World War it had reverted to the title Air Defence of Great Britain.

As the Battle of Britain opened Fighter Command had about 350 Hurricanes and 200 Spitfires as well as around 70 Blenheims and 25 Defiants.

Fighter Interception Unit – Established in April 1940, the unit's key purpose was the development of technology, including early airborne interception radar (AI). Equipped with Blenheims, Beaufighters and Hurricanes, the FIU saw action in the Battle. On July 23 an AI equipped Blenheim of the FIU shot down a Dornier Do 17 off Bognor Regis, said to be the first victory using airborne radar.

Film – The film, *The Battle of Britain*, was released in 1969 and was a broad historical portrayal of the Battle, for which a considerable fleet of aircraft was assembled for spectacular flying sequences, as well as scenes on the ground. Individual aircrew from the Battle were not specifically depicted.

Air Chf Mshl Dowding was played by Laurence Olivier and AVM Park by Trevor Howard, after Rex Harrison withdrew. Michael Redgrave portrayed AVM Evill. Other actors to have prominent roles included Michael Caine, Susannah York, Patrick Wymark, Christopher Plummer, Edward Fox, Robert Shaw, Ian McShane and Hein Riess as Goering.

Battle of Britain clasp holders who acted as advisers were Sqn Ldr Boleslaw Drobinski, Gp Capt Tom Gleave and Wg Cdr Bob Stanford Tuck. German advisers included Leutnant General Adolf Galland.

Fleet Air Arm – The Royal Naval Air Service was established on January 1 1914, though Naval flying had begun in 1909. Later in 1914 RNAS seaplanes patrolled as the British Expeditionary Force crossed to France. On April 1 1918 the RNAS and RFC amalgamated to form the RAF. For much of the period between the wars, naval aircraft were administered by the RAF, but operational control rested with the Navy. Between 1937 and 1939 the FAA was created as part of the Navy.

During the retreat to the Channel ports and evacuation of British and Allied personnel in 1940, FAA aircraft, flew sorties against the advancing Germans. For instance, Fairey Swordfish of No 812 Squadron, disembarked from HMS *Glorious*, launched two attacks on May 24 against an enemy column between Gravelines and Calais. Three tanks were claimed destroyed, for the loss to AA fire of one Swordfish and its crew, Lieutenant Ronald Carpmael and Lieutenant Kenneth Gurr.

Perhaps the most famous FAA operation took place on the night of November 11/12 when 21 Fairey Swordfish from HMS *Illustrious* attacked the Italian fleet in Taranto harbour in the south of Italy, causing much destruction.

The last Taranto survivor, Captain "Alfie" Sutton, died in 2008. As a Lieutenant he had been the observer in the aircraft flown by Lieutenant "Tiffy" Torrens-Spence which attacked the battleship *Littorio*. Altogether the ship was hit by three torpedoes and seriously damaged.

In February 1941 occurred the "Channel Dash" when the major German ships, *Scharnhorst*, *Gneisenau* and *Prinz Eugen*, with escorting vessels, sought to return to Germany from Brest. The limited British response included a suicidal attack by six FAA Fairey Swordfish of No 825 Squadron, led by Lieutenant Commander Eugene Esmonde.

The Swordfish took off from RAF Manston and, in daylight and with a far smaller fighter escort than had been envisaged, pressed home their attack despite the intervention of German fighters and intense fire from the ships.

All six Swordfish were shot down, though five men were rescued from the sea. The OC Manston, Wg Cdr Tom Gleave, a Battle of Britain veteran, wrote in his report, "I am of the opinion that Lieutenant Commander Esmonde is well worthy of the posthumous award of the Victoria Cross."

That award was gazetted 19 days later. Gleave would say that his view was accepted so readily that he deeply regretted not having recommended more VCs. However, of the survivors, the four officers received the DSO and the one rating, the CGM. Those who were killed were mentioned in despatches.

Esmonde had served in the RAF before the war, flying with No 43 Squadron. He then joined Imperial Airways. A great uncle, Major Thomas Esmonde, had earned the VC at the attack on the Redan (salient) at Sevastopol during the Crimean War.

As late as 1961 it was decided that two FAA squadrons should be included amongst the units which had taken part

Sub Lieutenant Henry Beggs was one of the Fleet Air Arm pilots to fly on attachment with Fighter Command. He joined 151 Squadron flying Hurricanes on July 1, was credited with destroying a Bf 109 on August 14 and, on August 15, was shot down and wounded. He returned to the FAA and was lost in 1942 when the aircraft carrier HMS Avenger was torpedoed and sunk west of Gibraltar with only 12 survivors.

in the Battle of Britain. They were No 804 Squadron (Sea Gladiators and Martlets) and No 808 Squadron (Fulmars flown solo).

More than 50 FAA pilots qualified for the B of B clasp, including those who flew on attachment with RAF squadrons.

Sub Lieutenant Dickie Cork, whilst serving with No 242 Squadron, was awarded the DFC. He correctly forecast that this would not be met with enthusiasm by the Admiralty, which substituted the DSC.

Fairey Swordfish on a training flight. (Courtesy of Imperial War Museum, London, negative no A 3532

Those lost whose bodies were not found, or who were buried at sea, are commemorated on the FAA memorial at Lee-on-Solent, Hampshire on which are the names of 1,400 FAA personnel from the Second World War who have no known grave.

Flypasts – On September 15 1945 the fifth anniversary of the Battle of Britain was commemorated by a flypast over London, in which a considerable number of veterans of the Battle participated, led by Douglas Bader. Others to fly included: Billy Drake, Pete Brothers, John Ellis, Frank Carey, Tim Vigors, Keith Lofts, Denis Crowley-Milling, "Hawkeye" Wells and Roy Bush. The formation also included No. 247 Squadron (which had taken part in the Battle) now flying de Havilland Vampires.

The flypast became an annual event. Tragedy struck on September 11 1953, when a rehearsal was being led by a Gloster Meteor flown by a Battle veteran, Wg Cdr Bobby Yule, OC RAF Horsham St Faith (now Norwich Airport). Above south east London another Meteor in the formation struck Yule's aircraft. It appears that, over a built up area, he made no attempt to escape, but instead tried to bring the crippled aircraft down amongst the buildings at the Royal Arsenal, Woolwich.

Bobby Yule died in the subsequent crash, despite attempts by Arsenal personnel to rescue him from the burning wreckage. In September 1993 a memorial to him was unveiled in the officers' mess at the Royal Arsenal by his two sons who had followed him into the RAF.

Growing concerns about the perceived dangers of flying Second World War aircraft over London led to the announcement that the 1959 flypast would be the last. During that event, a Spitfire flown by another of The Few, AVM Harold Maguire, forced-landed on the Oxo company sports ground at Bromley, Kent, just after cricketers had gone in for tea.

On September 15 1945 ACM Lord Dowding was photographed (centre of picture) at North Weald talking to Battle veterans who were about to take part in the flypast over London. Wearing the forage cap is Douglas Bader who had been present at the crucial meeting on October 17 1940. (Photograph courtesy Imperial War Museum London, negative no CH 16283)

Formations – Before the war rigid rules were laid down for the formations to be flown by Fighter Command and the "Fighting Area Attacks" to be employed in engaging enemy aircraft. These matters were much rehearsed and deviation from them was considered a serious transgression. One of the assumptions they were based on (which proved to be correct) was that, if war came, very inexperienced RAF pilots would be thrown into action.

Experience of battle (which the Germans already had from the Spanish Civil War) soon demonstrated the military maxim that no plan survives the first contact with the enemy. Some squadrons adapted quicker than others (or had COs more willing to disobey orders) and gave their aircrew more chance of surviving. In particular, the more enterprising RAF officers soon realised the vulnerability created by the standard formation of "Vics" of three.

A full squadron with 12 aircraft in two flights would consist of four Vics, usually flying line astern of the leader. At the beginning of an action the leader would indicate which standard attack was to be used.

The German experience in Spain resulted in the Luftwaffe adopting a looser fighter formation, based on what was called a Schwarm, consisting of four aircraft in the shape of outstretched fingers. Indeed, it became "Finger Four" formation to the RAF. Luftwaffe pilots were also encouraged to adapt to the situation in which they found themselves. They were aided by not having to worry constantly about the precision of their formation.

"I was still only 20. We'd lost a lot of the older chaps in France. We hadn't the experience of the German pilots like Galland who'd fought in the Spanish Civil War.

"So we'd fly around in pre-war Hendon pageant formations. The RAF hadn't had a Spain, nor the intelligence to learn from the tactics it produced. It hadn't kept pace with German thinking and the Gallands of the Luftwaffe." AVM "Birdie" Bird-Wilson, quoted in his *Daily Telegraph* obituary in 2001.

Gloster Gladiator – Bi-plane fighter, designed by Henry Folland, as an improvement on the Gauntlet. As the SS.37 it first flew in 1934 and began to enter service in 1937, despite fast approaching obsolescence. By the time of the Battle of Britain the type had already seen considerable service, including in France, the Norwegian campaign, Malta and (with the Finnish Air Force and Swedish Voluntary Air Force) the Winter War between Finland and the Soviet Union.

In the Battle, the Gladiator was flown by No 247 Squadron (from its re-formation on August 1 1940) and the Sea Gladiator variant by No 804 Squadron, FAA. The Gladiator was withdrawn from RAF service in 1944.

Ground crew – The gallantry of the ground crew who kept the fighters flying, sometimes under fire, has often been overlooked. Typically each aircraft would have its own airframe rigger and engine mechanic, while armourers, electricians and wireless mechanics would service a number.

Stories have circulated regarding an alleged "mutiny" at Manston on August 15, which, at their most colourful, involve an officer producing a gun to encourage recalcitrant ground crew out of a shelter. The evidence for the claims is limited and at least one officer who was at Manston that day has denied the substance of the story.

"Relationships with the pilots varied. Some would acknowledge their ground crews and have a bit of a chit chat,

Ground crew of No 222 Squadron with a Spitfire during the Battle. The photograph was taken by AC1 Joe Crawshaw.

others remained remote figures, but we always took a keen personal interest in our own pilot's welfare and would wait anxiously for his return from a sortie." Joe Crawshaw, an airframe rigger on No 222 Squadron.

"The ground crews were past all praise. If we had long hours, they had longer ones by far. They were always laughing and ragging around the place, betting cigarettes or drinks as to whether A flight would do better than B. A lot of publicity and glamour comes the way of the pilots, but not all the praise in the world would do justice to these back-room boys." Wg Cdr Mike "Red Knight" Crossley, CO of No 32 Squadron for part of the Battle, quoted by the *Daily Express*, 1990.

"The airfield was under attack and chunks of shrapnel were raining down. When I taxied towards dispersal no-one was to be seen; they were all in the airfield shelters taking cover.

Before I rolled to a halt and cut the engine, B Flight ground crew, under their Flight Sergeant, were swarming around my Spitfire, the bowser racing out to refuel the aircraft, while the armament men, laden with ammunition, were re-loading the guns.

"The noise from the explosions going on around us was terrifying, but not one of those magnificent men faltered in the tasks. I was frankly relieved to be taking off again." Sqn Ldr Ian Hutchinson, remembering being a Sgt Pilot on No 222 Squadron at Hornchurch.

"In September 1940, having been engaged in combat with ME 109s, during which my Spitfire was damaged, I came into land at Hornchurch airfield. As I touched down there was a twanging noise and both port and starboard ailerons drooped down.

"Whilst taxying towards my squadron dispersal I had time to reflect on the fatal consequences if the control wire, obviously hit by enemy fire, had failed as I came into land. As I parked my aircraft, still trying to relax, the senior NCO, i/c groundcrew greeted me with the curt comment, 'Now we have another unserviceable A/C'.

"No counselling in 1940!"

Sqn Ldr Cyril "Bam" Bamberger recollects the tribulations of being a Sgt Pilot on No 41 Squadron in 1940.

"Airmen's corner" at St Luke's Churchyard, Whyteleafe, Surrey, contains the graves of both aircrew and ground crew killed in the Battle. (Richard Hunting)

Group – The second tier in RAF command structure, with key functions being operational command and control. In Fighter Command in the Battle No 10 Group defended the south west and south Wales, No 11 south east England, including London, No 12 East Anglia and the Midlands and No 13 northern England and Scotland.

Guinea Pig Club – Club founded in June 1941 at the Queen Victoria Hospital, East Grinstead, Sussex, where RAF aircrew who needed reconstructive plastic surgery were under the care of the surgeon Archibald McIndoe (1900-1960, knighted 1947).

The name of the club, originally mainly for drinking, indicated the innovative nature of McIndoe's work and its existence highlighted his belief that badly disfigured men should enjoy as normal a life as possible and integration back into the community. Beer was provided on wards.

Men from the Battle of Britain who were early members included, John Fleming, Tom Gleave, Richard Hillary, Roy Lane, Geoffrey Page, "Ben" Bennions, Arthur Banham, Ralph Carnall, Roy McGowan, Patrick Wells and Bill Towers-Perkins, who was the first secretary.

Not all the members had suffered burns. Sgt Alan Morgan, for instance, was a Lancaster flight engineer in 1944 whose aircraft was hit by flak. He went to help an injured crewmate, became unconscious through lack of oxygen and lost all his fingers to frostbite. With McIndoe's help he spent his post-war career as a toolmaker.

The Club has wound down its activities in recent years as the number of members has declined.

"Ah, another bloody cripple! Welcome to the home for the aged and infirm!" The first words addressed by Richard Hillary to Geoffrey Page on the latter's arrival on the ward at East Grinstead.

"There was one man who was so bad his wife walked in and took one look at him and that was that – the end of the marriage." A Guinea Pig remembers. In some contrast, a former pupil of a local girls' school has recalled that she and her schoolmates were encouraged by teachers to wave to patients.

"His walk, which was usually rapid, had the slight rolling gait of a sailor. His humorous, twinkling eyes and enormous workmanlike hands were perhaps the most striking features of this unique man. Unique inasmuch as, apart from indefatigable skill as a surgeon, he had insight into human nature and a willingness to help that is rare." Geoffrey Page writes of Archie McIndoe in *Shot Down in Flames*.

> *We are McIndoe's army*
>
> *We are his Guinea Pigs*
>
> *With dermatomes and pedicles*
>
> *Glass eyes, false teeth and wigs*
>
> *And when we get our discharge*
>
> *We'll shout with all our might*
>
> *"Per Ardua Ad Astra*
>
> *We'd rather drink than fight"*

First verse of 'The Guinea Pig Anthem' – normally sung to the tune *Aurelia*, by Samuel Sebastian Wesley, often associated with the hymn, *The Church's One Foundation* by Samuel John Stone.

Geoffrey Page was one of the members of the Guinea Pig Club to return to action. Here, later in the war, Wg Cdr Page (second from left) briefs pilots before leading a sortie.

Hardest Day – Name sometimes given to Sunday August 18, when the German objective was to put out of action the airfields at Biggin Hill and Kenley. As part of the plan Dorniers flew at very low level across the Channel. They were not picked up by radar, but, as they crossed the coast at Cuckmere Haven, they were spotted by Observer Corps post K3 on Beachy Head. The plan failed, with Biggin Hill remaining operational and Kenley unusable for only two hours.

Some would argue for other "Hardest Days".

Hawker Hurricane – The fighter aircraft which accounted for the vast majority of Luftwaffe aircraft shot down in the Battle. Produced under the auspices of Hawker's Chief Designer, Sydney (later Sir Sydney) Camm, the prototype of this single seat and monoplane design first flew on November 6 1935.

In December 1937, No 111 Squadron, based at Northolt, became the first squadron to receive Hurricanes. A considerable publicity coup was achieved the following February when 111's CO, Sqn Ldr John Gillan, flew a Hurricane from Turnhouse (Edinburgh) to Northolt in 48 minutes at an average speed of about 409 mph. Official pronouncements did not dwell on the exceptional tail wind that had assisted this feat. However, in the RAF, the pilot became "Downwind" Gillan.

Hurricanes saw action in the "Phoney War" period and the Battle of France, with the first victory for the type being claimed by Pit Off "Boy" Mould of No 1 Squadron on October 30 1939.

Hurricane Mk 1s, as flown in the Battle of Britain, had Rolls Royce Merlin engines and four .303 in Browning machine guns in each wing.

In the Battle 35 Squadrons fought with Hurricanes. Pilots from that era recall a solid gun platform with a tight turning radius, capable of taking much punishment.

The aircraft would also see distinguished service, flying over Malta, the Western Desert and Burma. The Hurricat, catapult launched from ships, the Sea Hurricane and the "Hurribomber" were variants as was the "tank busting" version.

"To some extent the Hurricane was the Cinderella of the Battle of Britain. Everyone has heard of the Spitfire and accepts it as the victor of the Battle. This may have been due

This full size replica Hurricane stands at the National Memorial at Caple-le-Ferne. It depicts "Little Willie" of No 56 Squadron in which Geoffrey Page, the founder of the Memorial, was shot down on August 12. A replica Spitfire stands alongside. (Vic Seymour Photographic Services)

to its greater aesthetic beauty and finer aerodynamic form, or perhaps its admittedly higher performance." Air Chf Mshl Sir Christopher Foxley-Norris (a Hurricane pilot in 1940) in *A Lighter Shade of Blue*.

Head-on attacks – Amongst the pilots who developed the hair-raising technique of attacking German bomber formations head on were Sqn Ldr Mike Crossley of No 32 Squadron and Flt Lt Dennis "Bill" Armitage of No 266 Squadron. Sqn Ldr John Thompson of No 111 Squadron was also an advocate for this form of attack, as indeed was AVM Park. It was often utilised by Polish pilots. Very fine judgement was, of course, called for.

The theory was that you were firing directly at the key crew members; if you didn't shoot down an aircraft, you were at least likely to scatter the formation, making attacks by other RAF fighters easier and you might well send a damaged bomber limping back home with dead aircrew on board as a demonstration of what Fighter Command could do.

Not all pilots thought this concept was sensible and it certainly produced RAF casualties. Among those to be killed while flying head on at German aircraft were Fg Off Tom Higgs of No 111 Squadron on July 10, Fg Off Mike Ferris also of 111 on August 16 and Sqn Ldr Cedric Williams of No 17 Squadron on August 25. Higgs was the first Fighter Command airman to die in combat in the Battle.

Hellfire Corner – Loosely defined term in 1940, usually applied to all or part of the area taking in Folkestone and Dover, over or in sight of which so much fighting took place. The area was also within range of German guns.

In the First World War, the term was usually taken to refer to a crossroads on the Menin Road out of Ypres, often subjected to heavy German fire. After the war, the French placed many "demarcation stones" to mark the limit of the German advance in 1918 and one of the sites chosen was Hellfire Corner. The junction is now a roundabout.

Fg Off Mike Ferris of No 111 Squadron, who died in a head-on attack over Marden in Kent when his Hurricane collided with a Do 17. The German crew also died. Mike Ferris had been a member of the UAS at London University and a medical student at St Thomas's Hospital. (Family photograph via Edward McManus)

Home Guard – Established in May 1940 (then known as Local Defence Volunteers) as a force consisting of men whose age, health, occupation, etc made them unavailable for conventional military service. A key intention was that the LDV would act as guards and as observers of German movements, though many local commanders were determined to lead their men into action if an invasion took place.

In July the name of the force was changed to Home Guard, at least in part because Churchill believed that a more stirring name was needed.

The beginnings of the LDV/Home Guard had a chaotic element to them including lack of training, weapons and uniforms, but the force did much good work, despite being the butt of humour from the start.

The much-loved television programme, *Dad's Army,* milked the humorous side, but possibly part of the appeal of the programme is the underlying feeling that some of the real life Captain Mainwarings, Sergeant Wilsons and Private Godfreys would have, however suicidally, fought in the face of the German tanks if the situation had called for it.

During the Battle, German aircrew who arrived involuntarily in England were often greeted - and arrested - by Home Guard personnel. A Bf 109 pilot, after landing by parachute, noted with amusement the appearance on the scene of the local vicar, half in clerical garb and half in Home Guard uniform. One Home Guard veteran reminiscing in the 1950s was clearly far prouder of having taken part in such an episode than he was of his service in the Boer War.

Some Home Guard soldiers were trained to go into hiding behind German lines, in the event of invasion and harass the enemy.

Philip Ziegler recorded in his book, *London at War 1939-45,* that the maximum age for service was reduced from 68 to 66 in 1941. In the case of the 1st County of London Battalion, this led to the loss of one Duke, one Earl, one canon and six holders of the DSO.

Honours received by the force included standing guard at Buckingham Palace.

The Home Guard was disbanded in late 1944.

Hornchurch – Sector station D in 11 Group. The sector also took in the airfields at Hawkinge, Manston, Gravesend and Rochford. Hornchurch became operational in 1915, being originally known as Sutton's Farm.

Hostiles – Enemy aircraft.

Hurricane Burns – Pilots who were shot down in Hurricanes were statistically more likely to be killed or to suffer severe burns than those flying Spitfires. The positioning of a fuel tank was a factor and so was a lack of sealant between the wing fuel tanks and the cockpit in early aircraft. "Hurricane burns" became a piece of medical jargon.

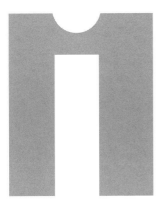

Ingram, Sir Bruce (1877-1963) – Proprietor and Managing Editor of the *Illustrated London News*, founded by his grandfather. He played a crucial role in establishing who had taken part in the Battle.

In July 1942, as Captain Ingram, he wrote to the Secretary of State for Air, comparing the importance of the Battle in British history with the defeat of the Armada and the Battle of Trafalgar. He argued that a permanent record of those who had played "an active part" should be created. He offered to arrange for the creation of a scroll with the names inscribed in gold leaf. This would be presented to Westminster Abbey or another institution.

While Sinclair, the Secretary of State, was supportive, the difficulties of undertaking the research in wartime were immediately noted, as was the problem of fairness in respect of the contribution made by many sections of the RAF.

On August 19 1942 the Air Council concluded that a roll of honour should be prepared of Fighter Command personnel killed in the Battle. This did not suit Ingram who wrote that the scroll should contain, "the names of the pilots of the fighter planes that went into the air to defend Britain, as it is obvious that one who came through the ordeal was just as great a hero as one who was killed in the action."

The official plan, however, proceeded and a scroll was prepared by the calligrapher, Daisy Alcock, which eventually included the names of both fighter and bomber aircrew lost during the Battle. This was presented to Westminster Abbey in 1947 at the same time as the Abbey's RAF chapel and Battle of Britain window were unveiled by the King.

Ingram, who edited the *Illustrated London News* for 63 years, was also a great supporter of and benefactor to the National Maritime Museum.

See also entry for Clasp.

Intelligence – German intelligence suffered from the diversity of the organisations tasked to provide it and the rivalry between them. Material produced by the main Luftwaffe intelligence organisation, headed by Oberst "Beppo" Schmid, varied from accurate to fanciful. A report in July 1940, for example, seriously under estimated British aircraft production and suggested that the only RAF fighter capable of taking on the Bf 110 was the Spitfire and then only in the hands of an excellent pilot. The report also failed to mention radar.

The intelligence provided, when put into practice, led to many lost opportunities. On August 13, Adler Tag, a number of airfields not in Fighter Command were listed for attack. The Coastal Command airfield at Detling, Kent was one that suffered badly, with 67 deaths including the station commander, Gp Capt Edward Davis, but this contributed little to the central objective of defeating Fighter Command.

Remarkably, the factory producing Spitfires at Woolston, Southampton, which was conveniently placed for the Luftwaffe, was not attacked until September 11.

British intelligence grew better as the Battle progressed, not least through the availability of German aircrew to interrogate. The Ultra device which enabled German Enigma codes to be understood provided some information to Fighter Command, though Dowding was only included in the Ultra "circulation list" in October.

Overclaiming of aircraft destroyed by pilots on both sides hampered accurate assessments of the situation and contributed to the Luftwaffe belief that it was winning the Battle.

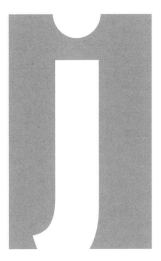

Jabo – Mission in which Bf 109s carried small bombs.

A bomb-carrying Bf 109E based in northern France in 1940 from where Jabo missions were carried out over Britain.

Jim Crow – Low level sortie over the English Channel to report details of incoming enemy formations.

Kenley – Sector station B in No 11 Group. The sector also took in the former (and future) civil airport at Croydon, slightly closer to London.

An operational airfield between 1917 and 1966, Kenley today is given over to housing and parkland. A memorial to the personnel who served there was unveiled in 2000 in a former E pen. In that year an English Heritage report described Kenley as the most complete surviving airfield from the Battle. It was designated a conservation area.

The Kenley memorial.
(Richard Hunting)

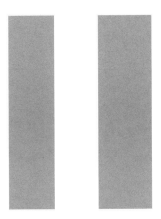

Leigh-Mallory, Sir Trafford Leigh (1892-1944) – Born in Mobberley, Cheshire. His father hyphenated his surname to Leigh-Mallory in 1914 and Trafford did the same, unlike his brother, George Herbert Leigh Mallory who, in 1924, with Andrew Irvine, may have been the first to reach the summit of Mount Everest, but neither survived.

Trafford Leigh-Mallory was educated at Haileybury College and Magdalene College, Cambridge. From 1914 he served in the Lancashire Fusiliers and then in France, where he was wounded, with the South Lancashire Regiment. In January 1916 he transferred to the RFC, qualified as a pilot and served with No 7 and No 5 Squadrons in France, using BE 2c two-seat biplanes to direct artillery fire.

Leigh-Mallory commanded No 15 (Reserve) Squadron and then No 8 Squadron, which flew the Armstrong Whitworth FK8 in close support of ground forces. A DSO was gazetted on January 1 1919. He was granted a permanent commission as a Sqn Ldr later in 1919. Between the wars his postings included CO of the School of Army Co-operation, instructor at the Army Staff College, attendance at the RAF Staff College, Andover, and SASO in Iraq.

His first experience of fighter operations came with his appointment in December 1937 to command No 12 Group with its headquarters in Nottinghamshire. Promotion to AVM followed 11 months later.

During the Battle Leigh-Mallory advocated the "Big Wing" plan as presented to him by Sqn Ldr Douglas Bader, CO of No 242 Squadron, whereas Park considered that wings took too long to assemble in the circumstances. Leigh-Mallory was claimed to have given No 11 Group in the front line too little support. Nonetheless, he replaced Park at No 11 Group in December 1940.

Together with Air Chf Mshl Douglas, who had replaced Dowding at Fighter Command, Leigh-Mallory was much criticised for the sweeps across the Channel in 1941, which resulted in many casualties. He later led Fighter Command, becoming an Air Mshl and he was appointed commander of the proposed allied expeditionary air force to support the liberation of Europe. He became an Air Chf Mshl in January 1944, having been knighted the year before.

As the plans for Operation Overlord developed and were implemented, Leigh-Mallory seemed excluded from the inner circle. In August 1944 he was appointed AO CinC, South East Asia Command, though American objections meant that he did not set off for three months. On November 14 the Avro York in which he was travelling with his wife crashed east of Grenoble, France and all aboard were killed.

Leigh-Mallory has suffered much adverse comment over the years and received some praise.

As far back as October 1938 Dowding had commented to Park (then his SASO) that a memo written by Leigh-Mallory, "shows a misconception of the basic ideas of fighter defence." Quoted in *Sir Keith Park* by Vincent Orange.

According to his brother George (quoted in *Big Wing: the biography of Air Chief Marshal Sir Trafford Leigh-Mallory* by Bill Newton Dunn), "He affects magnificence, rushing about in a splendid Crossley car and giving orders with the curt assurance of an Alexander the Great, or Lord Northcliffe or Rockefeller."

One of The Few, Wg Cdr Jock Thomson, speaking at the 1990 symposium, *The Battle Re-thought*, said, "Unlike Leigh-

Mallory, Park was a pilot's man, you felt you were speaking to a fellow tradesman." On the same occasion, the historian, Air Cdre Henry Probert commented, "Leigh-Mallory was not a team player, he was keen to make an impact in his own way."

However, Air Mshl Sir Denis Crowley-Milling, also a pilot in the Battle, praised Leigh-Mallory for his willingness to listen and to talk to pilots. Others have stressed his ability to work with the Army.

A problem, of course, is that Leigh-Mallory did not live to publish his own views.

Leigh-Mallory (right) with Dowding. (Courtesy Imperial War Museum, London, negative no CH 11054)

Local Defence Volunteers – see Home Guard

Locomotives – In 1941 the first of a class of revolutionary steam express locomotives entered service on the Southern Railway, to the design of its Chief Mechanical Engineer, O V S Bulleid. Features included an "air-smoothed" casing (leading to the nickname "spamcans" from the packaging for the wartime meat product) and unusual comfort for the footplate crew. The plan had been to name the class after British victories and a mock up nameplate, *The Plate*, was prepared commemorating the Battle of the River Plate in December 1939. However, with victories in short supply, the class was named after shipping companies that had used Southampton before the war and became the *Merchant Navy* class.

A smaller version, the *West Country* class, appeared in 1945, with names of cities, towns, villages and geographical features in the west of England. With the class spreading over the Southern system the decision was taken to give some names appropriate to the south east, including, *Fighter Command, Lord Dowding, Sir Keith Park, Biggin Hill, Hawkinge* and various aircraft and squadrons that had taken part in the Battle. One of this *Battle of Britain* class, *Winston Churchill*, hauled the former Prime Minister's funeral train in 1965 and is amongst those preserved.

Most of the locomotives named after squadrons carried the appropriate badge on both sides. By the time of the appearance of *66 Squadron*, the craftsman responsible had retired and badges were not fitted. The air smoothed casings were eventually removed from all the *Merchant Navy* locomotives and some of the others.

A number of Great Western Railway Castle class locomotives were named after RAF aircraft operational in 1940, including *Hurricane, Spitfire, Lysander* and *Fairey Battle*.

Luftwaffe – Generic German word for an air force. The term was used officially for the German air force as it existed in the Second World War (though not that which existed in the First World War) and is used again for the modern force.

Within the Luftwaffe were a number of operational commands, each one known as a Luftflotte (Air Fleet). In the Battle, the key Luftflotten confronted by the RAF were no 2 based in Belgium, The Netherlands and France, no 3 in France and no 5, flying from Norway. At least two combat

Hermann Goering (left) talking to the German fighter ace, Werner Molders. (Courtesy Imperial War Museum, London, negative number HU 4481)

Fliegercorps (flying corps) existed in each Luftflotte, which was divided into multiple units including the Geschwader (squadron, but much larger than an RAF squadron) in each of which fighters and bombers operated together. Gruppe (Group – conversely much smaller than its RAF equivalent) and Staffel (formation) were key sub divisions below Geschwader. A Staffel would have around 12 aircraft.

At the start of the Battle the Luftwaffe had just over 1,000 single seater fighters, about 350 two-seater fighters, almost 1,400 bombers and a little over 400 dive bombers. To counter this threat Fighter Command had approximately 750 single seater and 150 other fighters.

The Commander in Chief of the Luftwaffe was Hermann Goering (1893-1946) who had served in the German Army in the First World War and had then become an air force pilot, becoming commander of the Richthofen fighter unit and scoring a considerable number of victories. He was an early recruit to the Nazi Party and was wounded in the failed Munich "beer hall putsch" of 1923.

Goering rose steadily in the Nazi hierarchy and took command of the Air Force in 1935. His influence waned after his leadership failed to achieve the destruction of Fighter Command in 1940. The RAF's bombing of Germany and failures on the Russian front were other factors. After seeking to take over from Hitler in 1945 Goering was dismissed from his posts and arrested.

He was captured by American forces and put on trial at Nuremberg in 1946. He was found guilty of war crimes and sentenced to death, but committed suicide by poisoning.

Luftwaffe aircraft – The main combat aircraft operational with the Luftwaffe during the Battle were:-

Dornier Do 17: Bomber with a crew of four, or sometimes five, which could carry a bomb load of 1,000Kg. The 215 development was little used during the Battle, but because British intelligence had forecast that it would be in service by that time in considerable numbers, RAF pilots often reported attacking a 215 when in fact their target had been a 17.

Heinkel He 111: Bomber with a crew of four. Like the Dornier Do 17, it had participated with the Condor Legion in the Spanish Civil War, though an improved version was available in 1940. It carried 8 250kg bombs and proved to be particularly vulnerable when not escorted by fighters.

Junkers Ju 88A: A high speed bomber, which gained the respect of the RAF. It carried four crew members and a bomb load of up to 28 50kg bombs, plus 2 100kg bombs. Efficient and manoeuvrable and could sustain considerable battle damage, however defensive armament and armour were inadequate.

Junkers Ju 87B: Popularly known as the Stuka (German abbreviation for sturzkampfflugzeug – dive bomber), the aircraft was primarily intended for the direct support of ground troops. Its screaming dives could inflict considerable damage to morale, as well as the physical damage caused by its bombs.

"Being directly under a diving Stuka is an experience I do not wish to repeat," was the comment of one British soldier who spent two and a half days on the beach at Dunkirk before getting on to a ship.

In the Battle of Britain the Stuka proved vulnerable to attacks by single seater fighters and played little part in the later stages.

The Stuka carried a crew of two and one 500kg fragmentation or armour-piercing bomb.

Messerschmitt Bf 109E: The 109 was a single seat fighter which had also seen service in Spain. An outstanding aircraft, powered by a specially-boosted Daimler-Benz DB 601A engine and using direct fuel injection which was markedly superior to the carburettor feed of British opponents. It was armed with two machine guns in the fuselage and two cannon in the wings.

Known as the "Emil" in the Luftwaffe (they were "snappers" to the RAF), the 109E was generally considered the equal of the Spitfire and its superior at higher altitudes. It had a particularly cramped cockpit and limited fuel capacity, which sometimes forced it to leave bomber formations it was escorting. More physical effort was required to fly a 109 than either a Hurricane or Spitfire; on the other hand the 109E was the fastest of the three in a dive.

Variants were used in a fighter bomber "Jabo" role.

Messerschmitt Bf 110: Two seater fighter designed to carve a path for bomber formations through defences. Known as the "Zerstorer" (destroyer) it was powered by two Daimler-Benz DB 601A engines and had both machine guns and cannon.

The Bf 110 had good stability and manoeuvrability, but its lack of acceleration and speed were factors in the heavy losses it suffered in the Battle of Britain. Later in the war the 110 achieved success as a night fighter.

The designer of the 109 and 110, Wilhelm Emil "Willy" Messerschmitt (1898-1978), was perhaps the most famous of the German aircraft engineers, at least in the UK. His original work had been on gliders. He was imprisoned after the Second World War, then his company manufactured prefabricated buildings, small cars and sewing machines before returning to aircraft production. He remained Chairman of the Messerschmitt successor companies until 1970.

Until 1938 the company producing the Messerschmitt aircraft was known as Bayerische Flugzeugwerke, hence the official designation of the aircraft as "Bf". However, most people in Britain in 1940 referred to "ME 109s" and "ME 110s" and some sources claim that by that time they were right to do so.

In a post-war letter former Bf 109 pilot Joachim Schypek recounted the circumstances of his capture on October 25, during a Jabo escort mission. The Spitfire which shot him down was flown by Fg Off Peter "Sneezy" Brown of No 41

Squadron. Leutnant Schypek landed at Broom Hill near Lydd.

"To describe my last half mission, I must explain one thing first: we knew our position only very rarely. Usually we saw where we were heading but would not know just above which town we were any given time. So I think I must have been somewhere above Tunbridge Wells when we were attacked by Spitfires. However, I only know that we had been trying to reach London when we were intercepted and, of course, I know where I put my plane down.

"The 25th of October was a sunny day, rather chilly. I think number 6 Squadron had orders to carry bombs to London, the docks I assume, while 4 and 5 were assigned to escort 6. My usual position in the formation was in the rear to fly cover for the squadron as such.

"I forget which direction the Spitfires came from which engaged us, but there they were and when they threatened to come too close into our own rear I called out the agreed (warning?), 'Kniebeuge' (bend your knees!) which meant turn around 180 degrees. I started what I had practised successfully many a time before: I pushed my stick forward vehemently and went into a steep nosedive.

"Our Messerschmitt 109 Mark E had injection engines which ran smoothly independent from the flying position of the aircraft. Most of the Spitfires we met still had carburettor engines with floats that got stuck when the aircraft position was changed too violently (at least that was our explanation for the fact that our steep nosedives usually gained us a 300 to 400 metres extra distance from our pursuing Spitfires). I had been so successful with my manoeuvre so often that it was a very unpleasant surprise for me to note that the Spitfire grew even bigger in my rear view mirror.

"...I radioed that I was hit, that my aircraft was drawing big white vapour stripes, indicating I was losing cooling fluid fast, and that I would try to gain a safe distance from the English coast, expressing hopes that an air-sea rescue plane would pick me out of the Channel waters. 'What a nice gesture' I thought when a Spitfire passed alongside and the pilot – was he the one who shot me down, I don't know for sure – waved his hand at me and banked away.

"... When I eventually crossed the coastline near Lydd, about 11.15 Central European Time I was down to about 100 metres and too low to leave the three-mile zone off the English coast (our air-sea rescue planes had repeatedly moved that close to the coast.)... I headed for a free strip, jettisoned my cabin roof, put down the landing flaps fully and braced myself for the impact. However, it was much softer than I had anticipated.

"(A number of British soldiers led by a Captain ran up) He pulled out a check list and read out questions... he wanted to know whether my aircraft had a self-destruction gadget. It had none. Then he ordered me to surrender my revolver or pistol. I had only a Very pistol, which he wouldn't believe. It was against Luftwaffe orders, but I never carried one in the late days, they were too bulky for our small cockpits... "

Mae West – Colloquial name for lifejackets as worn during the Battle by RAF aircrew. Named after the well endowed American film actress. It was considered that a man wearing the jacket looked as though he had acquired a bust.

Some RAF aircrew believed that the German schwimmveste was better and utilised captured examples.

Pilots of No 610 Squadron at Hawkinge on July 29, Mae Wests much in evidence. Standing on the extreme left is Plt Off Stan Norris, who, later the same day, forced-landed in a Spitfire damaged in combat. Standing fourth from the right is Sgt Norman Ramsay. July 29 was his 21st birthday. Both survived the war. (Courtesy Imperial War Museum, London, negative no HU 1062)

Memorials – The National Memorial to The Few at Capel-le-Ferne, Kent was unveiled by HM Queen Elizabeth the Queen Mother in 1993. Other major memorials, specific to the Battle include the Battle of Britain Memorial Chapel and window in Westminster Abbey (1947) and the Monument on London's Embankment (2005).

The Runnymede Memorial by the Thames was inaugurated by HM The Queen on October 17 1953. On it are the names of RAF aircrew lost during the Second World War, with no known grave, who were based in the UK and countries of northern and eastern Europe. Those whose bodies were recovered and then formally buried at sea are included. The names of many men from the Battle of Britain are to be found.

Designed by Edward Maufe (knighted in 1954 for services to the IWGC), the memorial was built on land donated by Sir Eugen and Lady Millington-Drake. Sir Eugen had played an important part in a celebrated incident from the early days of the war. He was Minister to Uruguay at the time of the Battle of the River Plate in December 1939 and had therefore been an important figure in the diplomatic manoeuvring that culminated in the scuttling of the German pocket battleship, *Admiral Graf Spee*.

Many small memorials have appeared over the years, often specific to a particular person. For example, Whitbread Road in Ludlow, Shropshire is named after Plt Off Laurence "Hops" Whitbread of No 222 Squadron (KIA September 20) - though the practice of illuminating the parish church of St Laurence on the anniversary of his death has ceased - and a small memorial stands at the roadside near Newlands on Romney Marsh, close to where a Hurricane flown by Plt Off Arthur Clarke of No 504 Squadron crashed on September 11. Arthur Clarke's remains were discovered at the crash site years after the war and left where they lay at the request of his family.

In 2006 the Shoreham (Kent) Aircraft Museum launched a project to provide memorials at all the sites within 10 miles of the museum where Fighter Command aircraft crashed during the Battle and aircrew were lost.

Particularly charming (if historically inaccurate) wording is to be found on the small plaque on the churchyard wall at Brenchley, Kent:-

"To the undying fame of the gallant lads who fought the Battle of Britain over this corner of England in August-September 1940 and to the glorious memory of those who then gave their lives. Per Ardua ad Astra."

In cases where the body of a Battle of Britain airman was available to be buried in the UK, families might have chosen to use an existing family grave or provide their own stone for a new grave or utilise an IWGC (CWGC from 1960) headstone. In some cases the official headstone was placed on an existing family grave. An example of this is to be found at Macclesfield Cemetery, Cheshire, where lies Sgt Eric Bann of No 238 Squadron (KIA September 28).

At Treyford, West Sussex, just off the South Downs Way, stands a small memorial erected by the family of a German airman killed on August 13, Adler Tag. Oberleutnant (though the memorial says Hauptmann) Josef Oestermann was the pilot of a Ju 88 attacking the airfield at Farnborough, Hampshire. After intervention by a number of Hurricanes, the rest of the crew – Unteroffiziers Rosler and Seitz and Obergefreiter Brieger – baled out and were taken prisoner. Oestermann was still in the aircraft when it crashed at Treyford and no trace of him was found.

"In ever loving memory of our darling elder son 'Tony', Colin Anthony Hobson, Pilot Officer 600 Squadron, RAF. Born October 25 1918, killed October 3 1940. Never was so much owed by so many to so few (Churchill)." Inscription on family gravestone in the churchyard of All Saints, Banstead, Surrey.

"He died in glory fighting for freedom." Part of the wording on the headstone of Plt Off Dennis Holland of No 72 Squadron, in the churchyard at Chaddleworth, Berkshire.

The headstone on the grave in which Sgt Fred Eley is buried in St Margaret's churchyard, Wrenbury, Cheshire. Sgt Eley, a Spitfire pilot with No 74 Squadron, was killed in action on July 31 1940. The date on the stone is incorrect. (Photograph, David Moores)

"Dutchy" Holland was shot down on September 20 and died soon after. He was 23.

Merlin – The engine that powered both the Hurricane and Spitfire throughout the Battle. Originally developed, in the inter-war period, by Rolls Royce as a private venture (under the name PV 12), it had 12 cylinders in a vee configuration and displaced 27 litres. Many thousands were produced during the war and the Merlin later powered the Mosquito, Lancaster and the American P-51 Mustang, which had Merlins built under licence by Packard in the United States. The enemy Messerschmitt Bf 109E also had a V12 engine, the Daimler-Benz 601A, but in this case it was installed the other way up, with the vee open at the bottom.

One of the signs of American support for Britain in 1940 was the supply of 100 octane fuel which enhanced the performance of the Merlin, leading, in particular, to greater climbing ability for Hurricanes and Spitfires.

Rolls Royce produced a number of aero piston engines named after birds. In ornithology the Merlin is a falcon, smaller than the kestrel, which, in Britain, lives in open countryside and young forestry plantations. Interestingly, the first Messerschmitt 109 prototype was powered by a Kestrel engine.

Mess Bills – A standard response from members of The Few when asked for their feelings on hearing Churchill say, "Never in the field of human conflict was so much owed by so many to so few" is, "We thought he was talking about our mess bills." This is said to come from a comment at the time of the speech by Sqn Ldr Mike Crossley of No 32 Squadron, who warned his men that the Prime Minister must have been studying their bills.

Middle Wallop – Sector station Y in No 10 Group. Situated south west of Andover, Hampshire and officially operational (though uncompleted) from June 12. Other stations in the sector, used by Fighter Command during the Battle, were Warmwell, Boscombe Down and Chilbolton. Both the USAAF and FAA were later users of Middle Wallop.

Today Middle Wallop is HQ of the Army Air Corps. The Museum of Army Flying is on the site.

Millionaires' Squadron (or Millionaires' Mob) – Nicknames for No 601 (County of London) Squadron, AAF, which flew Hurricanes in the Battle. Some of its pilots were wealthy and it was also a particularly socially prominent squadron, even for the AAF. This is perhaps illustrated by the fact that during the Battle it was commanded by Sqn Ldr the Hon Max Aitken (son of Lord Beaverbrook), Sqn Ldr the Hon Edward Ward (son of the Earl of Dudley) and Sqn Ldr Sir Archibald Hope Bt. One of its personnel was Flt Lt William Rhodes-Moorhouse (KIA September 6), son of the first air VC (1915).

The Squadron was officially formed at Northolt on October 14 1925, though early members were given to claiming that

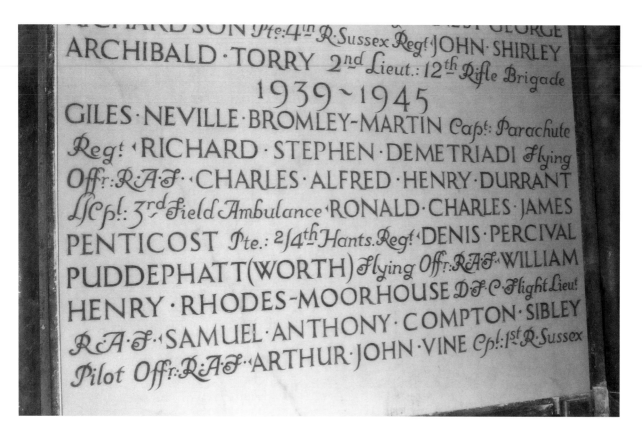

RICHARDSON Pte: 4th R. Sussex Regt JOHN SHIRLEY ... GEORGE
ARCHIBALD · TORRY 2nd Lieut.: 12th Rifle Brigade
1939~1945
GILES · NEVILLE · BROMLEY-MARTIN Capt: Parachute
Regt · RICHARD · STEPHEN · DEMETRIADI Flying
Offr: R.A.F · CHARLES · ALFRED · HENRY · DURRANT
L/Cpl: 3rd Field Ambulance · RONALD · CHARLES · JAMES
PENTICOST Pte.: 2/4th Hants. Regt · DENIS · PERCIVAL
PUDDEPHATT (WORTH) Flying Offr: R.A.F · WILLIAM
HENRY · RHODES-MOORHOUSE D.F.C. Flight Lieut!
R.A.F · SAMUEL · ANTHONY · COMPTON · SIBLEY
Pilot Offr: R.A.F · ARTHUR · JOHN · VINE Cpl: 1st R. Sussex

Two pilots killed in the Battle with No 601 Squadron are remembered at St Martin's Church at Westmeston, Sussex. The family home of Fg Off Dick Demetriadi was in the area, though his brother in law, Flt Lt Willie Rhodes-Moorhouse, was interred at his family home in Dorset. Dick Demetriadi's body was buried in France. (Photograph Edward McManus)

it had actually been formed at White's Club, St James's. The first CO was Lord Edward Grosvenor.

Ministry of Aircraft Production – Set up in 1940 by Churchill to improve the flow of aircraft to the RAF and FAA in particular. RAF storage units, accused of being slow to issue aircraft to squadrons, were also taken over. The first Minister was Lord Beaverbrook, who adopted working methods not usually associated with the Civil Service, but presided over an improvement in the rate at which squadrons received new aircraft. The Ministry was merged into the Ministry of Supply during 1945 and 1946.

Mitchell, Reginald Joseph (1895-1937) – Born in the Staffordshire village of Butt Lane, the son of a headmaster, R J Mitchell began his career with the locomotive manufacturer Kerr Stuart. He moved on to the Supermarine Aviation Works at Woolston, Southampton, where he became Chief Designer at the age of 24, with the title of Chief Engineer added shortly afterwards.

Mitchell developed Supermarine's reputation as a manufacturer of flying boats, but also achieved great success, with a succession of designs, in the Schneider trophy races.

In 1928 Vickers acquired Supermarine and part of the deal was that Mitchell would remain with the organisation for five years.

Today Mitchell is most remembered for his association with the Supermarine Spitfire. He brought to bear his experience of high speed flight and co-ordinated the work and ideas of a number of engineers to produce one of the most successful military aircraft of all time.

For four years before his death Mitchell was seriously ill with cancer.

There are two plaques on his birthplace at 115 Congleton Road, Butt Lane. In late 2008, the nearby Reginald Mitchell Primary School announced plans for a museum in the designer's honour. The *Sentinel* newspaper quoted headteacher Alan Stancliffe as saying, "We've got history on our doorstep and don't celebrate it enough. People visit Shakespeare's birthplace and celebrate it, so why not here?"

The bust of R J Mitchell in the RAF Club, Piccadilly, London. (RAF Club)

Morrison, Herbert (1888-1965) – Joined the Independent Labour Party in 1906 and steadily rose to the heights of socialist politics. He became secretary of the London Labour Party in 1915, Mayor of Hackney in 1920 and Labour Party Chairman in 1928/29. His first spell in Parliament began in 1923 as member for South Hackney. In 1934 he became leader of the London County Council.

When Labour entered the wartime coalition government Morrison was appointed Minister of Supply. He replaced Anderson as Home Secretary in October 1940. Like his predecessor he had a shelter named after him. The Morrison shelter, introduced in 1941, was designed following evidence that people did not make use of purpose-built shelters. The Morrison was made of very heavy steel and could be put in the living room and used as a table. Two or three people could sleep in them.

Despite seeking to supplant Attlee as leader of the Parliamentary Labour Party after the 1945 General Election, Morrison was made Lord President of the Council and Deputy Prime Minister. He was later Foreign Secretary.

Nationalities – The contribution of men from many parts of the world was vital in winning the Battle of Britain.

Inevitably, the debate continues on the nationality of some of those who took part, but the broad picture was provided by Kenneth Wynn in *Men of the Battle of Britain* who suggested that the figures from outside the UK were:-

Australia 33, Belgium 29, Canada 98, Czechoslovakia 88, France 13, Ireland 10, Jamaica 1, Newfoundland 1, New Zealand 126, Poland 145, the Rhodesias 3, South Africa 25, United States 11.

The funeral of Plt Off Billy Fiske at The Priory Church of St Mary and St Blaise in the village of Boxgrove close to Tangmere airfield. In 2008 the 601 Squadron Old Comrades' Association dedicated a window in the Priory to the memory of Billy Fiske. (via www.bbm.org.uk)

Different designs of CWGC headstones denote different nationalities. Here in St Illogan's churchyard, Illogan, Cornwall is the grave of Flt Lt Miroslav Kredba who was killed in a flying accident on February 14 1942. Kredba had escaped from Czechoslovakia when the Germans arrived, had then served with the French Air Force and escaped again to Britain, where he joined the RAF. He flew in the Battle of Britain, as a Plt Off, with No 310 Squadron, the unit he was with at the time of his death. (Edward McManus)

The list appended at the end of the film *The Battle of Britain* included one Israeli, despite the fact that the State of Israel did not come into being until 1948. This presumably referred to Plt Off George Ernest Goodman of No 1 Squadron, who was born in Haifa, in what was then the British Mandate of Palestine, in 1920. He held a British passport.

One of the American volunteers, Plt Off Billy Fiske of No 601 Squadron, had attracted a great deal of attention, because of his wealth, social standing and sporting achievements, before joining the RAF in 1939. He was badly burned on August 16, after his aircraft was hit by return fire and died the next day.

It is often claimed that Fiske was the first American to die in British service in the Second World War, but that is disputed. There is evidence that Flt Lt Jimmy Davies, lost while flying with No 79 Squadron on June 27, held American citizenship. Certainly his, British, fiancée believed him to be American. However, the CWGC lists him as British.

In 1941 a tablet in memory of Billy Fiske was unveiled in St Paul's Cathedral by Sir Archibald Sinclair. It reads:-

"Pilot Officer William Meade Lindsley Fiske 111, Royal Air Force, An American citizen who died that England might live. August 18th 1940." The date is incorrect.

Specifically designated national squadrons operational in the Battle were:-

No 1 (RCAF),

Poland – No 302, No 303

Czechoslovakia – No 310, No 312.

Newall, Sir Cyril Louis Norton (1886-1963) – Born in India, attended RMA Sandhurst and was commissioned (in 1905) into the Royal Warwickshire Regiment, as were at least two other military leaders of the Second World War, Montgomery and Slim.

Newall saw service on the North West Frontier and, in 1911, transferred to the 2nd Gurkha Rifles. Having learnt to fly in 1911, he gained his RFC wings in 1913. Initially an instructor, he was promoted to Major in 1915 and, later in the year, took command of No 12 Squadron, leading it in France.

On January 3 1916, Newall led three Cpls into a burning shed containing many bombs and played a key role in removing bombs and extinguishing the fire. He received the Albert Medal in Gold. In 1971 living holders of this award were invited to exchange it for the GC. He later commanded a training wing in the UK and wings and a brigade in France.

After the war Newall was granted a permanent commission in the RAF as a Gp Capt. He commanded the school of technical training for apprentices at Halton and served at the Air Ministry. As an AVM in the early thirties he was head of RAF Middle East, based in Cairo. He was then Air Member for Supply and Organisation. In 1935 he became KCB and was promoted to Air Mshl.

In September 1937 Air Chf Mshl Newall was appointed CAS, despite the claims of at least three other possible candidates including Dowding. In this post Newall demonstrated a determination to make the RAF ready for war and a belief that Britain could best be defended by having a powerful bomber force for counter offence.

However, Sir Thomas Inskip, Minister for Co-ordination of Defence, espoused the theory that the priority was a strong fighter force capable of resisting German bombers. Newall was supported by Viscount Swinton, Secretary of State for Air, in his opposition to Inskip, but the latter won the argument in Cabinet. Newall's consolation was that he managed to gain authorisation for higher expenditure, which ensured that the work of making the RAF ready for war in the short term could move forward alongside long term expansion plans.

Newall regarded the Munich agreement of 1938 as a national humiliation and re-doubled his efforts to make ready for conflict.

When war came he was forced to commit bombers, fighters and army co-operation units to operations across the Channel, against his own judgement. He resisted pressure from the other services to bomb Germany, following the invasion of Norway, but changed his position as the Blitzkreig began, proposing successfully that attacks on the Ruhr should begin.

Often attending Cabinet meetings, Newall played a key role in preventing the despatch to France of more Hurricanes, desperately needed for the defence of Britain.

Newall objected to the creation of the Ministry of Aircraft Production in May 1940 and inevitably came into conflict with Beaverbrook. At the same time his view that Dowding should be replaced later in the year at Fighter Command brought him into conflict with the Prime Minister.

In addition Newall had lost the support of Lord Trenchard, "Father of the RAF", who though retired still wielded considerable influence. Trenchard was an enthusiast for taking the offensive at every opportunity and for strategic bombing as a means to win wars.

All this led to political skulduggery to undermine CAS. In the summer of 1940 an anonymous memo was widely circulated which called for a new holder of the post and declared, "Air Chief Marshal Newall is not the best man: indeed as CAS he is a real weakness to the RAF and to the Nation's defence." Various claimed personal weaknesses of Newall were listed including lack of judgement and foresight.

It is now known that the memo was written by Wg Cdr Edgar James Kingston-McCloughry, then serving at the Air Ministry and the author of a book published in 1937, *Winged*

Warfare – Air Problems in Peace and War. In addition, Kingston-McCloughry fed information to Beaverbrook, gained some access to Beaverbrook's social circle and fuelled his anti-Newall position. Beaverbrook was also seeking to acquire more of the Air Ministry and to influence the choice of the next CAS.

Newall ceased to be CAS on October 24. The intrigue had damaged him and he gave some the impression of mental

Sir Cyril Newall – "prime architect of the wartime air force". This painting, executed in 1940, is by Reginald Grenville Eves. (Courtesy of Imperial War Museum London, negative no LD 762)

weariness, but he had served a significant period in the post at an exceptionally difficult juncture.

Promotion to MRAF and admission to the OM followed and he became Governor-General of New Zealand in 1941, serving until 1946. He earned much respect there and stood determinedly against the country's government on one occasion on a point of principle. He became a Baron in 1946.

Newall disliked contact with the media and did not write memoirs. His contribution to preparing the RAF for the Battle of Britain has, partly for those reasons, rarely been highlighted.

To MRAF Sir John Slessor (CAS 1950-52), Newall was, "the prime architect of the wartime air force".

Nicknames – Nicknames for aircrew were often seen as a sign of being accepted and frequently stayed with the person concerned for life.

There were plays on names – "Polly" Flinders, "Bunny" Currant, "Sticky" Glew, "Robin" Hood.

Some described a personal habit – "Social Type" Jeff was always immaculate. "Broody" Benson would, between sorties, sit slumped in a chair. "Tannoy" Reid was often to be heard on the radio.

Some referred to physical appearance – "Woolly Bear" Ritchie was big, but also gentle; "Sawn-off" Lock was small; "Dopey" Davies was supposed to look like one of the Seven Dwarfs.

Others were biographical – "Dimsie" Stones had been caught with the book by Dorita Fairlie Bruce, *Dimsie Goes to School*. "Sailor" Malan and "Sinbad" Inniss had both been to sea before joining the RAF. "Sheep" Gilroy had been a farmer and "Sticks" Gregory a professional drummer. For "Hawkeye" Wells the origins of his nickname lay with his achievements as a schoolboy shooting champion in New Zealand. He continued to demonstrate his talent while flying RAF fighters.

"ICK. D.S.O.:D.F.C.   41 SQUADRON

"Sawn-off" Lock as portrayed by Cuthbert Orde. During the Battle "Lockie" as he was also known, was awarded the DFC and bar and by the end of 1940 he had the DSO too. He was one of the considerable number of veterans of the Battle shot down during the fighter sweeps over France in 1941 and has no known grave. (Courtesy Imperial War Museum, London, negative number LD 2363)

"Grubby" Grice, "Widge" Gleed and "Fanny" Brinsdon were among those who claimed not to know the reasons for their sobriquets. For the slight Gleed the name appears to have been an abbreviation of "Wizard Midget".

Three Battle veterans (left to right), Billy Drake, Bob Stanford Tuck and Bobby Yule about to take part in a Battle of Britain flypast in Singapore in 1948. In 1940 on No 257 Squadron, Flt Lt "Cowboy" Blatchford was apparently the only person with the nerve to refer to Tuck as "Beaky", a name derived from the re-designing of Tuck's face in a pre-war flying accident. Blatchford was a Canadian devotee of Hillbilly music. (Courtesy Gp Capt Billy Drake)

In the case of Billy Drake, "Billy" was neither a nickname nor a diminutive. It was his given name.

Northolt – Sector station Z in No 11 Group, which also included the Group's HQ at Uxbridge. Opened in 1915 for the RFC.

In early 2009, RAF Northolt, officially considered a "Core Defence Site", was in the process of expanding. Among its residents was No 32 (The Royal) Squadron – a Hurricane squadron in the Battle.

North Weald – Sector station E in No 11 Group. The airfield became operational in 1916. Other stations in the sector were Stapleford Tawney and Martlesham Heath. The North Weald Airfield Museum is a modern reminder of 1940.

Observer Corps – Established in 1925, the Observer Corps grew out of the experience gained in defending London in the First World War and the work of Major General Edward Ashmore. At first it was under the command of the Army, but transferred to the control of the Air Ministry in 1929. During the 1930s the Corps expanded to cover much of the UK. From 1936 the Corps HQ was at Bentley Priory as part of Fighter Command.

During the Battle of Britain, the Corps played a key role in the reporting of enemy aircraft. At its most basic in that era a post consisted of a platform surrounded by sandbags.

A particularly dramatic moment occurred at 4.16pm on September 7 when the Observer Corps centre at Maidstone received a report of "many hundreds" of enemy aircraft approaching the Kent coast – the first mass attack on London was underway.

Dowding, in his despatch on the Battle of Britain, wrote: "It is important to note that at this time (the Observer Corps) constituted the whole means of tracking enemy raids once they had crossed the coastline. Their work throughout was quite invaluable. Without it the air raid warning systems could not have been operated and inland interceptions would rarely have been made."

On April 9 1941 approval was given by the King for a change of title to The Royal Observer Corps. In the same year women took operational roles for the first time.

The Corps was stood down on May 12 1945, re-formed in 1947 and, after service in a nuclear defence role, stood down again in 1992, following the end of the Cold War. Its badge depicted one of the Elizabethan beacon lighters recruited to give warning of approaching danger.

Off duty – For The Few life was often a contrast between days spent fighting for their lives and evenings and nights spent in London clubs or country pubs, sometimes in the company of wives and girl friends.

On September 15, Plt Off "Chas" Frizell, a Canadian serving with No 257 Squadron, was a passenger in a car which, in the blackout, struck an anti invasion obstacle while returning from the pub to Martlesham Heath, Suffolk. The car behind, driven by the CO, Sqn Ldr Bob Tuck, crashed into the back. As a result Frizell spent three months in hospital.

One respected flight commander led a sortie that was bounced, leading to four deaths including his own. His comrades felt that he would have been more alert had he not spent the previous night with his girl friend.

"There was, however, a lighter side. On many evenings we managed to sample the local ales, particularly at the Old Greyhound in Croydon, where the chef provided us with the rare treat of rump steak. My parents lived in south London and I was able to see them sometimes." Wg Cdr Bob Foster breaks off from an account of combat with No 605 Squadron in the Battle.

There were plenty of pubs that became popular with off duty fighter aircrew – most famously, those stationed at Biggin Hill and Kenley would often assemble in the White Hart in the village of Brasted, near Westerham. Many of them signed the blackout board, which is now in the keeping of the Shoreham Aircraft Museum.

"Taxying out to form up for take off I often turned on the oxygen which seemed to clear the head and was ideal for the effect of a hangover." Sqn Ldr "Joe" Leigh.

"I had my Bugatti and my Matchless motorcycle with me at Coltishall and took them out whenever I could, enjoying the peace and quiet." Commander Jimmy Gardner, RN, who served on No 242 Squadron – quoted in his *Daily Telegraph* obituary.

Plt Off Charles Upton (left) and Plt Off Anthony Woods-Scawen in a moment of relaxation. They were great friends. (Courtesy Mrs "Bunny" Ford, who, as "Bunny" Lawrence, was Anthony's fiancée)

Pancake – Instruction to return to base. It could also refer to a wheels-up landing.

Parachutes – Many British aircrew had little training in using a parachute at the time of the Battle which may have contributed to the number of fatalities.

In addition, there were well founded fears amongst aircrew that they might be shot at under their parachutes, so that sometimes men delayed deploying the chute.

An incident involving No 87 Squadron took place on August 11, when Plt Off Dennis David managed to fight off two Bf 109s attacking the wounded Plt Off John Cock as he came down by parachute off Portland Bill. Cock swam ashore at Chesil Beach.

As the dying Sgt Bert Black of No 46 Squadron lay in hospital he told his wife Gwen how RAF fighters had protected him while he was under his parachute. Black was a Fairey Battle pilot who had volunteered for Fighter Command.

On September 15 Sgt Leslie Pidd of No 238 Squadron was killed under his chute by German fire. In a letter the next day his comrade, Sgt Eric Bann, wrote, "now after seeing poor Pidd go shall I ever forgive the Hun".

Ironically, less than two weeks later, Bann would die when his chute failed to open.

A counter view was taken by Air Chf Mshl Dowding, who commented in his 1941 despatch:-

"Germans descending over England are prospective prisoners of war and, as such, should be immune. On the other hand, British pilots descending over England are still potential combatants.

"Much indignation was caused by the fact that the German pilots sometimes fired on our descending airmen (although in my opinion they were perfectly entitled to do so), but I am glad to say that in many cases they refrained and sometimes greeted a helpless adversary with a cheery wave of the hand."

Park, Air Chief Marshal Sir Keith Rodney (1892-1975)

Park, Air Chief Marshal Sir Keith Rodney (1892-1975) – Born in Thames, North Island of New Zealand. Served with NZ artillery at Gallipoli. He transferred to the Royal Artillery and then the RFC and from 1917 flew Bristol Fighters with No 48 Squadron in France, commanding the squadron from April 10 1918. He was awarded the MC and bar and DFC.

Inter-war appointments included service at HQ Air Defence of Great Britain, command of No 111 Squadron and of RAF Northolt.

As a Gp Capt he was Air ADC to the King from January 1937 and became OC RAF Tangmere in December that year. In July 1938 Air Cdre Park became SASO at Fighter Command. With the rank of AVM he became AOC No 11 Group, Fighter Command on April 20 1940 and held this command throughout the Battle of Britain. He was moved to an Air Training post in December 1940, leading many to claim that his contribution to winning the Battle was not appreciated. He returned to operational duty, serving in the Middle East and Malta and as Air C in C, South East Asia Command.

He was retired from the RAF in 1946, a decision which he categorised as "a very great disappointment and a shock".

Much of his later life was spent in New Zealand; he held posts in aviation and supported charities.

Park has been described as tougher than Dowding when it came to removing those who failed to perform. He had few close friends and did not enjoy socialising outside his family. He could appear aloof, yet could also deploy great charm.

In early 2009 it appeared likely that a statue of Park would be erected in Central London.

"If ever any one man won the Battle of Britain (Park) did. I don't believe it is realised how much that one man, with his leadership, his calm judgement and his skill did to save not only this country but the world." MRAF Lord Tedder, CAS, speaking at the annual dinner of the New Zealand Society in London, February 1947.

"What Park achieved in the Battle of Britain is in itself enough to place him amongst the great commanders of history. But his performance in 1940 was not a one-off. In 1942 in Malta Park took the offensive and turned Kesselring's defeat into a rout. After that he directed the air operations that enabled Slim to expel the Japanese from Burma. He was as adept at offence as he was at defence and, like Wellington, he never lost a battle. His record makes him today, without rival, the greatest fighter commander in the history of air warfare." Stephen Bungay, *The Most Dangerous Enemy.*

"The awesome responsibility for this country's survival rested squarely on Keith Park's shoulders. Had he failed, 'Stuffy' Dowding's foresight, determination and achievement would have counted for nought." Gp Capt Douglas Bader, a Battle veteran, addressing the memorial service for Park on September 12 1975, at St Clement Danes Church, London.

Phases – Most historians agree that the Battle had a number of phases, though there is not always total agreement on their dates and form. Typically it might be argued that the phases were:-

July 10-August 7 – fighting over the sea

August 8-23 – Lead up to Adler Tag, the day itself and its aftermath

August 24-September 6 – Attacks on airfields, chain home stations and aircraft factories

September 7-30 – The emphasis of the attacks switches further inland, notably including London

October 1-31 – The Battle fades. Attacks at night and high level sorties which attempt to take Fighter Command aircraft beyond acceptable operational ceilings

It is sometimes claimed, with justification, that August 8 was actually the last day of the first phase, given that its main feature was the fighting over Convoy CW9 in the Channel.

Pile, Major General Sir Frederick Alfred Bt (1884-1976) – Entered bottom of his term at RMA, Woolwich, 1902. Battery commander in RHA during the retreat from Mons, 1914, later being awarded the DSO and MC. In the 1920s he started a long spell in the Royal Tank Corps. In 1937, as a Major General, he took command of the 1st Anti-Aircraft Division (TA), defending London. In July 1939 he assumed the leadership of Anti-Aircraft Command and held the post until April 1945, being promoted General in 1941. He enjoyed a close relationship with Air Chf Mshl Dowding.

After the war Pile was Director General of Housing at the Ministry of Works and then went into industry.

His nickname of "Tim" was arbitrarily bestowed by the wife of an early CO.

"That afternoon (August 14) there were further raids by small formations on Southampton, Bristol, Portland and Cardiff and when night fell it was clear that the defenders had given a good account of themselves, for the day's total by anti-aircraft fire amounted to eight destroyed and five damaged. Dowding rang me up to congratulate us. I thanked him but said that the congratulations were really entirely due to Fighter Command and the man who had trained them. Dowding then said simply, 'Pile it's a miracle – the miracle of the Marne over again. The pilots were wonderful, but it was a miracle.'" From Sir Frederick Pile's memoir, *Ack Ack*.

"It was a measure of his success that he kept the Prime Minister's confidence in all the crises of the Battle of Britain, the night Blitz, and the concluding attack by pilotless aircraft and rockets in 1944–5." Kenneth Macksey in the *Oxford DNB*.

Portland, Battle of – At about 09.45am on Sunday August 11, Ventnor chain home station reported a large German force developing over the Cherbourg Peninsula. A major attack on the Portland naval base followed, the most important feature of a day in which the RAF suffered its worst aircrew casualties of the Battle of Britain, with 25 killed.

The fighting became known as "The Battle of Portland". The original event of that name was the three days of fighting in the Channel in 1653, between British and Dutch ships, the former commanded by General at Sea Robert Blake.

Radio Direction Finding (Radar) – The deficiencies of the First World War defences against aerial attack and the oft-repeated theory that "The bomber will always get through" led to much scientific activity between the wars. One result of this was the "sound mirrors" erected in Kent in the 1930s, which, in exercises, proved to be virtually useless in the vital task of detecting incoming "enemy" aircraft and giving useful information about them.

A committee to explore scientific means of aiding home defence was established, under the chairmanship of Henry Tizard.

"Death rays" to kill aircraft crews were considered, from the point of view of eliminating what was realised to be an impractical idea. Robert Watson-Watt of the National Physics Laboratory was asked to investigate and one of his staff, A F Wilkins, pointed to knowledge that already existed on the impact of aircraft on radio beams.

This led to an experiment in 1935 whereby an RAF Handley Page Heyford bomber was flown in the direction of the BBC transmitters on Borough Hill outside Daventry, Northamptonshire. A radio beam was displaced by the aircraft to an extent that was measurable.

A radio direction finding experimental unit was then established at Orfordness, Suffolk, headed by Watson-Watt. Later nearby Bawdsey Manor was purchased and lattice masts constructed.

The inevitable setbacks and disagreements occurred, but, after considerable progress, it was decided, in 1935 that 20 stations should be established; later the term "chain home" was applied to them. The first – at Bawdsey – became operational in 1936. By early 1940 29 stations were available, covering a considerable portion of the UK.

Although most chain home stations were on the coast, a few were well inland, such as Stoke Holy Cross in Norfolk and Ottercops Moss in Northumberland. "Chain Home Low" stations also came into play, detecting aircraft at particularly low levels.

The most visible equipment of a station in the Battle consisted of very tall transmitter and receiver masts.

The term "Radar" was in limited use at the time of the Battle. The German "Freya" system was relatively sophisticated, but mainly used in 1940 to find targets at sea for artillery.

"In addition to the Observer Corps, there is another means of obtaining information of the enemy's approach. I regret that I can not give you much information about this system because its existence is very secret and I must specially ask all present here today not to refer outside this college to the existence of this organisation which has been christened 'RDF'.

"Suffice it to say that by this means (which has superseded the 'sound mirrors' previously relied on) we are able to detect the approach of aircraft over the sea up to a distance of 60 miles or more and, in the absence of any congestion, to plot their courses with fair accuracy."

From lectures delivered by Air Chf Mshl Dowding in May 1937 at the Imperial Defence College and the RAF Staff College.

Ranks – RAF and Luftwaffe ranks were not precisely equivalent. Some examples of approximate equivalents are:-

Sergeant = Unteroffizier, Unterfeldwebel

Flight Sergeant = Feldwebel

Warrant Officer = Stabsfeldwebel, Oberfeldwebel

Pilot Officer = Leutnant

Flying Officer = Oberleutnant

Flight Lieutenant = Hauptmann

Squadron Leader = Major

Wing Commander = Oberstleutnant

Group Captain = Oberst

Readiness – Readiness was the most advanced state of preparedness for a squadron and meant that it was available to take off in a very short time. "Available" was one step down from this and also meant that the squadron could take off in a specified number of minutes. Sometimes part of a squadron would be at "Readiness", part at "Advanced Available" and part at "Normal Available". "Released" meant that a squadron was not required until a specified time. Sometimes "Stand-by" was used, which indicated that pilots were required to be seated in the cockpit with the aircraft pointed into the wind, but the engine off.

Royal Auxiliary Air Force – See entry for Auxiliary Air Force.

Royal Air Force Volunteer Reserve – Organisation established in 1936 to recruit men from a wide range of social backgrounds and referred to by the Air Ministry as a "democratic reserve of aircrew for use if war should come". It would provide about 780 of the pilots who flew in the Battle of Britain, including some who had previously served in earlier bodies, such as the Civil Air Guard and the F Reserve.

From the outbreak of war the RAFVR became the principal vehicle through which RAF aircrew were recruited.

One of the pre-war members of the RAFVR, without whom the Battle could not have been won. Plt Off Robert Jones flew Hurricanes with No 605 Squadron. On Black Thursday, August 15, he shot down an He 111. He is shown here as a Sergeant. (via www.bbm.org.uk)

The organisation exists today in much changed form – for example providing officers who administer the ATC.

"Without the RAFVR the Battle could not have been won." Dr Tony Mansell, article *Who Were The Few?* In *1940* magazine, no 1, 2001.

Royal Canadian Air Force – No 1 Squadron RCAF flew Hurricanes in the Battle. Its first base in the UK was Middle Wallop in June, but it did not become operational (from Northolt) until August.

In 1941 the squadron was renumbered No 401, being effectively part of the RAF, although still nominally an RCAF unit.

Royal Observer Corps – See entry for Observer Corps.

Saul, Air Vice Marshal Richard Ernest (1891-1965)

– Served in the RFC in First World War, qualifying as a pilot and commanding No 4 Squadron on the Western Front. Between the wars his postings included a spell in Iraq and as Commandant of the School of Army Co-operation. He became SASO, No 11 Group in 1937 and, in July 1939, AOC, No 13 Group, covering the North and Scotland. During the Battle he pursued a policy of only sending experienced squadrons south as replacements, which was shown to minimise casualties.

In February 1941 Saul moved to No 12 Group. He later commanded Air Defences, Eastern Mediterranean. He retired from the RAF in 1944, and held a senior UN post.

Scores – Though numbers of enemy aircraft destroyed by individual RAF pilots are often quoted and "league tables" produced, a variety of factors militate against accurate accounting. Official figures were not published; some pilots would over claim and a few under claim; often several pilots attacked – and claimed as destroyed – the same aircraft; intelligence officers might be inclined or disinclined to allow a claim; there may or may not have been witnesses, such as other squadron members, the crew of a ship reporting an aircraft or parachute going into the sea, or an Observer Corps post seeing a falling aircraft or descending parachute; the pilot who claimed the victory may or may not have had the opportunity or the desire to follow his victim down; on some units the higher your rank, the more your chance of being credited with a kill; there was a theory that sometimes it was no bad thing to let a badly damaged bomber with bloody remains on board escape as a warning to the others – and so the list goes on.

In *Battle of Britain: The Hardest Day,* Alfred Price drew attention to the case of the Ju 88 that crashed into woods, close to the church at Ide Hill, near Sevenoaks, Kent at about 1.30pm on August 18. Oberfeldwebel Eichhorn and his crew were killed. Price calculated that a total of 4.5 was added to the scores of various RAF pilots as a result of the fall of this aircraft.

Generally, being credited officially with five enemy aircraft destroyed was seen as the qualification for being regarded as an "Ace". This status would most likely lead to the award of the DFC to an officer and, quite possibly, the DFM to an NCO.

Sgt Josef Frantisek, a Czech serving with the Poles of No 303 Squadron, is often regarded as the highest scoring RAF pilot of the Battle, despite being killed on October 8. Kenneth Wynn in *Men of the Battle of Britain* gives him 17 victories.

Among the other high scoring pilots in the Battle were: Flt Lt "Sammy" Allard, No 85 Squadron; Flt Lt Pete Brothers, No 32 and No 257 Squadrons; Fg Off Brian Carbury, No 603 Squadron; Sqn Ldr Michael Crossley, No 32 Squadron; Plt Off Bob Doe, No 234 and No 238 Squadrons; Fg Off John Dundas, No 609 Squadron; Fg Off Colin Gray, No 54 Squadron; Sgt Jim Hallowes, No 43 Squadron; Fg Off Pat Hughes, No 234 Squadron (KIA September 7); Sgt "Ginger" Lacey, No 501 Squadron; Plt Off Eric "Sawn-Off" Lock, No 41 Squadron; Sgt Andrew McDowall, No 602 Squadron; Sqn Ldr Archie McKellar, No 605 Squadron; Fg Off Desmond McMullen, No 54 and No 222 Squadrons; Sqn Ldr Bob Tuck, No 92 and No 257 Squadrons; Flt Sgt George "Grumpy" Unwin, No 19 Squadron; Plt Off Charles Upton, No 43 and No 607 Squadrons; Fg Off Witold Urbanowicz, No 145 and No 303 Squadrons; Flt Lt "Pancho" Villa, No 72 and No 92 Squadrons.

Success in the Battle came to the RAF because, whatever the true scores on each side, the Germans eventually realised that they were not going to knock out Fighter Command and achieve air superiority.

"At 29,000 feet P/O Broadhurst and myself engaged some ME 109s. I delivered a quarter attack on one ME 109 opening fire at 200 yards and ceasing fire at 30 yards. I fired seven bursts at him and on my second white smoke commenced to pour from his engine. This got thicker and black smoke mingled with it as he went down. I could see flames from his engine cowling as I followed him down, but at 20,000 feet, having followed him from 29,000 feet, I was attacked by another ME 109 and was forced to leave him." A combat

Sergeant Josef Frantisek of No 303 Squadron, as drawn by Cuthbert Orde. (Courtesy of Imperial War Museum, London, negative number LD 421)

This Bf 109E forced-landed at Love's Farm, Marden, Kent on September 5. Oberleutnant Franz von Werra was taken prisoner. He would later escape from Canada and become the subject of the book and film, The One That Got Away. The victor was Plt Off "Stapme" Stapleton of No 603 Squadron, although soldiers manning a Lewis gun at a searchlight unit also tried to claim the credit. (Kent Messenger PD1463472)

report from Sgt Ian Hutchinson of No 222 Squadron illustrates the difficulty of keeping score.

Perhaps the last word on this subject should go to Air Chf Mshl Sir Christopher Foxley-Norris, a long serving Chairman of the BBFA. Thinking, in 2000, of the less successful pilots he wrote, "—- the fact that they were there and played their part decisively tipped the balance in our favour."

Scramble – order to take off immediately.

"The worst time was just waiting. When the phone rang ——- the orderly would shout 'squadron scramble – angels 15'. In an instant we were running to our aircraft, grabbing the parachute off the wing, buckling it on as you scrambled into the cockpit. Then pull on the helmet already attached to radio and oxygen supply, whilst somehow starting the engine. It was a grass field without runways, so it's a matter of getting into the wind, keeping a sharp lookout for other aircraft, full throttle and away we go." Flt Lt Denis Robinson who fought with No 152 Squadron at Warmwell, Dorset.

Sea – On the British side rescue of aircrew from the sea at the time of the Battle was not the highly organised operation that it later became. Around 140 airmen went into the sea and have no known grave.

In contrast, probably the only man who survived two duckings in the Channel was Flt Lt Christopher Deanesly of No 152 Squadron. On July 25 (as a Fg Off) he was hit by return fire and wounded; he ditched south of Portland and was picked up by the SS *Empire Henchman*. On September 26 he was shot down south of The Needles in combat with Bf 109s and baled out wounded. This time he was rescued by an RN launch. Some who knew the extrovert Deanesly felt that he amply justified his nickname of "Jumbo" and found surprising his ability to leave a Spitfire cockpit in a hurry.

Plt Off "Pip" Cardell of No 603 Squadron. On September 27 he died despite the efforts of his friend Plt Off Peter Dexter.

On September 27, Plt Off "Pip" Cardell of No 603 Squadron baled out wounded off Folkestone, but his parachute did not open. Plt Off Peter Dexter of 603, having failed to attract the attention of people on shore, landed on the beach at Folkestone and commandeered a boat. He found Cardell dead.

During the battle over Convoy CW9 on August 8 a Hurricane flown by Sgt Kenneth Smith of No 257 Squadron fell into the sea off St Catherine's Point on the Isle of Wight. Two days later, in a broadcast by Lord Haw Haw, it was claimed inaccurately that Smith was a PoW. This led his mother to become convinced that he would one day walk back through the door and his belongings were left untouched. Sgt Smith is remembered on the Runnymede Memorial.

German arrangements for the rescue of downed airmen were more advanced. However, Fighter Command aircrew were under orders to attack German rescue aircraft. For example, on August 8 Sqn Ldr Fenton of No 238 Squadron destroyed a He 59 float plane. His aircraft was, however, hit by return fire. Fenton was injured in ditching and was picked up by the trawler *Basset*, under naval command.

On October 26 Fg Off Donald McHardy and Plt Off Geoffrey Simpson of No 229 Squadron were shot down by Bf 109s while attacking an He 59. Simpson was killed and McHardy captured.

Sea Lion, Operation (Seelowe, Unternehmen), –

German hopes that, after Dunkirk, Britain would seek some kind of accommodation came to nothing and preparations for Operation Sea Lion, the invasion of Britain, began.

The theory was that the Luftwaffe would destroy the fighting ability of the RAF and thus achieve air superiority over the English Channel and Southern England. The Luftwaffe would also deal telling blows to the Royal Navy, whose threat would be eliminated, once its key bases were in German hands. A British Army which had left men and vast

Opposite, bottom: Dover on May 31. A Royal Navy destroyer arrives with troops from Dunkirk. Incidents that day included the loss of the motor boat, Janis, which suffered a direct hit from a bomb off Dunkirk Pier, the tug Lady Rosebery, hit and blown up with the loss of two crew including 15-year-old Ordinary Seaman John Edward Atkins and the adventures of the Leigh-on-Sea cockle boats, Endeavour, Letitia, Reliance, Renown, Defender and Resolute, which, sailing together off Gravelines, managed to survive an attack by a large force of German bombers. (Courtesy of Imperial War Museum, London, negative number H1637)

Above: *Royal Engineers disembarking at Dover during the Dunkirk evacuation. One appears to have acquired either a souvenir or a makeshift weapon. (Courtesy Imperial War Museum, London, negative number H 1618)*

amounts of equipment in France would be no match for the German forces crossing the Channel in barges under an air umbrella.

On July 16 Hitler issued a directive which gave as an aim the elimination of "the English motherland as a base from which war against Germany can be continued and, if necessary, to occupy the country completely." A further directive on August 1 demanded the final conquest of England, with invasion envisaged on September 15. On August 2 Goering issued his orders to the Luftwaffe for a rapid victory over the RAF.

On September 19, with Fighter Command still very much in being and winter approaching, Hitler reduced the priority of Sea Lion as an immediate objective and on October 12 he ordered that preparations for invasion were to be seen only as a means of exerting pressure on Britain.

September 7 – The Saturday on which the Germans launched the first mass attack on London – the beginning of the Blitz. Various factors led to this decision, including the belief that Fighter Command's final reserves could be destroyed if they were forced to defend the capital and the perceived need to save face after Bomber Command had attacked Berlin.

With continued bombing of London from that date Fighter Command airfields and other previous targets were attacked less –in the opinion of some, including participants, this was a major factor in the survival of the Command as an effective force. The Germans had failed to stick to their prime objective.

Huge fires were started by the bombs on the east side of London, including in the Surrey Docks and the Royal Arsenal at Woolwich and nearly 500 people on the ground were killed. The worst conflagration that night was in Quebec Yard in the Surrey Docks, rated officially as a "300 pump" fire. A "200 pump" fire amongst explosives and live ammunition was tackled at the Arsenal.

The Prime Minister in the East End on September 8, in the hours after the first major Luftwaffe attack on London. (Courtesy of Imperial War Museum, London, negative number H 3978)

"We kept close formation until we reached Woolwich and then we saw an extraordinary spectacle. There was nothing but fire ahead, apparently stretching right across the river and burning on both its banks. We seemed to be entering a tunnel of fire – no break in it anywhere. All the usual landmarks were obliterated by the walls of flame. Burning barges drifted past. For many hours no contact with the shore was possible. We did what we could where we could as we slowly worked our way up river." The leader of a group of fireboats, quoted in *Firemen at War* by Neil Wallington.

Shepley Spitfire The – On June 29, Plt Off Douglas Shepley of No 152 Squadron, a Cranwell graduate, married Miss Frances "Bidy" Linscott. They were both 21.

Douglas Shepley had already lost two siblings since the outbreak of war. His sister Jeanne, a Volunteer in the ATS, had died on October 18 1939 when the SS *Yorkshire* of the

Bibby Line, sailing from Rangoon to Liverpool, was torpedoed and sunk about 800 miles west of Bordeaux by U-37.

On May 31, Flight Lieutenant George Rex Shepley was the pilot of a Lysander of No 16 Squadron shot down over Dunkirk.

On August 12, Douglas was one of two 152 pilots killed in an action south of the Isle of Wight, the other being Flt Lt L C "Elsie" Withall.

Bidy and her mother in law, Emily, determined to raise the money to replace the Spitfire that Douglas had been flying.

Plt Off and Mrs Shepley on their wedding day, June 29 1940. (Family photograph)

With the support of Lord Beaverbook, Minister of Aircraft Production and helped by collections in all the ARP posts in Sheffield, £5700 was raised in less than four months. On August 16 1941 *The Shepley Spitfire* was issued to No 602 Squadron. It was lost on March 28 1942 while being flown by Gp Capt Victor Beamish, a Battle of Britain veteran.

In 1979 the *Shepley Spitfire* pub was opened in the village of Totley, outside Sheffield, close to the Shepley family home. The first pint was pulled by Seymour, another brother of Douglas.

Sinclair, Sir Archibald Henry Macdonald Bt (1890-1970) – After Eton and Sandhurst Sinclair joined the Life Guards in 1910. He succeeded to the Baronetcy in 1912, on the death of his grandfather. "In the days before the First World War there were few more glamorous young men in Society," according to the *Oxford DNB*. During this period he flew - and formed a close friendship with Churchill. For four months on the Western Front he was Churchill's second in command with the 6th Battalion, Royal Scots Fusiliers. Between 1919 and 1921 he was successively Churchill's personal military secretary at the War Office and his private secretary at the Colonial Office.

In 1922 Sinclair was elected Liberal MP for Caithness and Sutherland. After being Liberal Chief Whip and Secretary of State for Scotland in the National Government led by Ramsay MacDonald, he became Chairman of the Parliamentary Liberal Party in 1935. In September 1939 he declined an offer from Neville Chamberlain, then Prime Minister, to take office. Following Churchill gaining the Premiership on May 10 Sinclair became Secretary of State for Air, finding himself in conflict with the empire-building Lord Beaverbrook, Minister of Aircraft Production. In addition Dowding blamed him both for failing to stand up to Churchill in the matter of extra Hurricanes being sent to France and in connection with the change of leadership of Fighter Command in November. Sinclair had visited

Duxford and listened to No 12 Group complaints about the alleged failure to use the "Duxford Wing". On November 13 he had met Dowding and told him of the intention to remove him from Fighter Command.

Sinclair retained his post until 1945 and lost his Parliamentary seat in the General Election of that year. He was created Viscount Thurso in 1952.

Slaughter of the Innocents – A description applied to Friday July 19 when No 141 Squadron flew from West Malling into action for the first time in Defiants. Over the Channel six aircraft were shot down by an enemy which had come to understand the aircraft's limitations. Ten aircrew were killed and two wounded.

In the Biblical book of Matthew the term is applied to the alleged killing of the children of Bethlehem on the orders of King Herod – although there appears to be little historical evidence to confirm the event.

Some Mother's Son – The (in 1940) controversial words on an anonymous wreath sent to the funeral of Leutnant Walter Binder, whose Bf 109 crashed into gardens between Ann Street and Robert Street, Plumstead on August 31. The aircraft's destruction was credited to Sgt Jack Stokoe, flying a Spitfire of No 603 Squadron.

At about the same time, another No 603 Squadron Spitfire crashed on Woolwich Common with the loss of Fg Off Robin Waterston. Claims that the Bf 109 hit Waterston's aircraft, leading to its demise, have been refuted by witnesses.

"I watched the Messerschmitt fall from a great height. It didn't strike another aircraft on the way down." Mrs Joyce Simpson, then Joyce Lill, an 18 year old civil servant.

Squadron – A loosely defined RAF administrative unit. A single seat fighter squadron at the time of the Battle, at full strength, might have had just over 20 pilots and 15 aircraft.

A fighter squadron then was normally divided into A Flight and B Flight with the colours red, green, blue and yellow used to denote sections.

The 71 squadrons and other units that officially took part in the Battle were as follows. All were under the control of Fighter Command.

1, 1 (RCAF), 3, 17, 19, 23, 25, 29, 32, 41, 43, 46, 54, 56, 64, 65, 66, 72, 73, 74, 79, 85, 87, 92, 111, 141, 145, 151, 152, 213, 219, 222, 229, 232, 234, 235, 236, 238, 242, 245, 247, 248, 249, 253, 257, 263, 264, 266, 302, 303, 310, 312, 501, 504, 600, 601, 602, 603, 604, 605, 607, 609, 610, 611, 615, 616, 804 (FAA), 808 (FAA), plus 421 Flight, 422 Flight and the Fighter Interception Unit.

Three squadrons, 235, 236 and 248, were attached to Fighter Command from Coastal Command.

Some squadrons received equipment donations and other support from particular regions or countries, resulting in a name being incorporated in their titles. Examples were: No

Opposite:
The Air Council in session in the Council Chamber at in July 1940 at Adastral House, London. Left to right: AVM A G R Garrod; Sir Harold Howitt; Air Mshl Sir Christopher Courtney (Air Member for Supply & Organisation); Air Mshl Leslie Gossage (Air Member for Personnel); Captain H H Balfour (Under Secretary of State for Air and Vice President of the Air Council); Sir Archibald Sinclair Bt (Secretary of State for Air and President of the Air Council); Air Chf Mshl Sir Cyril Newall (Chief of the Air Staff); Sir Arthur Street (Permanent Under Secretary of State for Air); Air Chf Mshl Sir Wilfred Freeman (Air Member for Development and Production); Sir Charles Craven (Civil Member for Development and Production); and Flt Lt W W Wakefield (Parliamentary Private Secretary to the Parliamentary Under Secretary of State for Air). (Courtesy of Imperial War Museum, London, negative no CH 966)

56 (Punjab), No 79 and No 264 (Madras Presidency) and No 249 (Gold Coast).

Station Commanders – Officers commanding a fighter station were normally Gp Capts or Wg Cdrs.

Some were unable to resist seizing opportunities to go into action. They included Gp Capt Stanley Vincent of Northolt – who became probably the only RAF pilot credited with destroying enemy aircraft in both World Wars – Wg Cdr Johnny Dewar (Exeter), who was killed by the enemy, but in unexplained circumstances, on September 12 and Wg Cdr Victor Beamish of North Weald. Dewar, a former test pilot, was the highest ranking RAF officer killed in the air during the Battle of Britain.

Supermarine Spitfire – In the Battle the Spitfire equipped 19 squadrons. The Supermarine Chief Designer R J Mitchell was responsible for creating the Spitfire and the aircraft was flown for the first time from Eastleigh aerodrome (now Southampton Airport) by Captain Joe "Mutt" Summers on March 5 1936. After Mitchell's death in 1937, Joe Smith was promoted to Chief Designer and headed the team responsible for the development of the aircraft.

The name Spitfire was suggested by a director of Vickers-Armstrong (the Supermarine parent company), Sir Robert Maclean, who used the Elizabethan expression, "a little Spitfire", to describe his daughter Ann. This name had also been applied unofficially to a previous Mitchell design.

It is claimed that Mitchell commented, that it was, "just the sort of bloody silly name that they would choose". However, if the Air Ministry had had its way, the aircraft would have become the Supermarine Shrew.

The Spitfire entered RAF service with No 19 Squadron in 1938 and served, in a variety of roles and with major improvements throughout the war. The last operational Spitfire sortie was flown by No 81 Squadron in Malaya in 1954.

Famous for its looks, achievements and the sound of the Merlin engine which powered many Spitfires, the aircraft nonetheless shot down far fewer enemy aircraft in the Battle of Britain than the Hurricane, which was in service in greater numbers at the time. Most Spitfires in the Battle were equipped with eight .303 Browning machine guns. There were a few carrying cannon.

The Naval version was known as the Seafire.

"The Supermarine Spitfire remains one of the classic fighter aircraft of all time, and certainly one of the most instantly recognizable. In the United Kingdom it has become a part of folklore – the aeroplane that saved the United Kingdom in the Battle of Britain. The fact that reality tells a different story does not diminish the psychological impact it has had over the years." From the website of The Spitfire Society.

"When Mutt shut down the engine and everybody crowded round the cockpit, with R J [Mitchell] foremost, Mutt pulled off his helmet and said firmly, 'I don't want anything touched.' This was destined to become a widely misinterpreted remark. What he meant was that there were no snags which required correction or adjustment before he flew the aircraft again. The remark has crept into folklore implying that the aeroplane was perfect in every respect from the moment of its first flight, an obviously absurd and impracticable idea." Jeffery Quill in his book, *Spitfire*. At the time he was assistant to Summers and was present.

"The Spitfire was a useful aircraft in that an idiot could fly it." Sqn Ldr Gerald Stapleton, a Battle veteran, quoted in *Stapme* by David Ross.

Tally ho! – An indication from the leader of an RAF formation that he had sighted enemy aircraft. The expression has been used in hunting from the 18th century to announce that the hounds have seen the fox. It may come from 'taiaut', a French word with a similar meaning.

Tangmere – Sector station A in No 11 Group, with Westhampnett (later the Goodwood motor racing circuit) also in the sector.

The airfield was opened late in the First World War by the RFC and used initially for training.

Today, the Tangmere Aviation Museum movingly evokes the Battle period.

Test Pilots – Test pilots from Hawker and Supermarine flew in the Battle to assess aircraft in combat.

Flt Lt Richard Reynell, an Australian, was a member of the RAFO at the outbreak of war, but remained on secondment to Hawker. On August 26 he was attached to No 43 Squadron at Tangmere. On September 2 he claimed a Bf 109 destroyed, believed to be that flown by Leutnant Riegel (reported missing), which was hit over Ashford, Kent. Five days later Reynell was lost during the defence of London against the first major Luftwaffe attack. At about 4.45pm his Hurricane fell on Blackheath, south east London. Reynell baled out wounded and landed nearby, but was dead when found.

In the same engagement 43 lost its CO, when Sqn Ldr Caesar Hull, a South African and close friend of Reynell, was shot down, his Hurricane falling in the grounds of Purley High School.

Fg Off Jeffery Quill of Supermarine flew with No 65 Squadron between August 6 and August 24, claiming on the 16th, the destruction of a Bf 109. The squadron was based at Hornchurch, but often moved forward to Manston. During his attachment Quill was invited to talk to Lord Beaverbrook, Minister of Aircraft Production, about cannon. However, according to Quill's recollections, his attempt to pass on his views was abandoned with the Minister asleep. Quill did return to Supermarine with knowledge that was used to improve the Spitfire.

He and Reynell were friends, having served together in the Meteorological Flight at Duxford before the war.

A replica of a Spitfire flown by Quill, while with No 65 Squadron, stands at the National Battle of Britain Memorial at Capel-le-Ferne.

Other test pilots to see action in the Battle included Flt Lt Noel Hall (No 257 Squadron) and Flt Lt Johnny Kent (No 303 and No 92 Squadrons), both of whom had served at the RAE, Farnborough. On August 8 "Henry" Hall was lost during the Battle of Convoy Peewit off St Catherine's Point on the Isle of Wight. His body was found by the Germans and he is buried in France.

The Few – An expression which has become a shorthand tribute to the aircrew of Fighter Command in the Battle. It is based on a passage in a speech made by Winston Churchill in the House of Commons on August 20, in which he said:-

"The gratitude of every home in our Island, in our Empire, and indeed throughout the world, except in the abodes of the guilty, goes out to the British airmen who, undaunted by odds, unwearied in their constant challenge and mortal danger, are turning the tide of the world war by their

From left to right are, Sqn Ldr "Dave" Glaser, Fg Off Ken Wilkinson, Wg Cdr Vivian Snell, Flt Lt Les Harvey and WO Antoni Markiewicz. Flying with the Polish Air Force on September 1 1939, Markiewicz may have been the first person to destroy a German aircraft in the war. Sadly, in the spring of 2009, Ken Wilkinson was the only survivor of this group. (Courtesy Battle of Britain Fighter Association)

Many of The Few had joined the RAF before the war on short service commissions. Flt Lt Ian Hallam was one of those. He was an Army Co-operation pilot who volunteered for Fighter Command and flew with No 610 and No 222 Squadrons in the Battle. He was killed in a flying accident in 1952, as a Sqn Ldr.

prowess and by their devotion. Never in the field of human conflict was so much owed by so many to so few."

However, it is often claimed that Churchill was referring to RAF aircrew in general, or to both Bomber and Fighter Command personnel. Although the thrust of his remarks, in the lead up to the famous paragraph (after referring to various major contributions to the war effort) had been about fighters, he had also alluded to bombers and he went on to say:-

"All hearts go out to the fighter pilots, whose brilliant actions we see with our own eyes day after day; but we must never forget that all the time, night after night, month after month, our bomber squadrons travel far into Germany, find their targets in the darkness by the highest navigational skill, aim their attacks, often under the heaviest fire, often with serious loss, with deliberate careful discrimination, and inflict shattering blows upon the whole of the technical and war-making structure of the Nazi power. On no part of the Royal Air Force does the weight of the war fall more heavily than on the daylight bombers who will play an invaluable part in the case of invasion and whose unflinching zeal it has been necessary in the meanwhile on numerous occasions to restrain."

How the words were perceived at the time was indicated by Air Chf Mshl Dowding when he departed from Fighter Command in November 1940. He sent a letter to stations and units under his command in which he wrote:-

"My Dear Fighter Boys

"In sending you this, my last message, I wish I could say all that is in my heart. I cannot hope to surpass the simple eloquence of the Prime Minister's words, 'Never before has so much been owed by so many to so few.' The debt remains and will increase.

"In saying good bye to you I want you to know how continually you have been in my thoughts and that, though our direct connection may be severed, I may yet be able to help you in your gallant fight.

"Good bye to you and God bless you all."

The speechmaker himself gave a firm view. *In The Second World War, Volume II, Their Finest Hour*, Winston Churchill, wrote, "At the summit (of endeavour in the Battle of Britain) the stamina and valour of our fighter pilots remained unconquerable and supreme. Thus Britain was saved. Well might I say in the House of Commons, 'Never in the field of human conflict was so much owed by so many to so few.'"

The Few are remembered in many parts of the world. Here on column 240 of the Alamein Memorial in North Africa is the name of Flt Lt James Julius Frederick Henry Bandinel who was posted missing as a Hurricane pilot with No 260 Squadron in December 1941. Bandinel had been at Charterhouse School and then went up to Oriel College, Oxford, where he joined the UAS. In the Battle of Britain, Plt Off Bandinel flew Hurricanes with No 3 Squadron. (Photograph Edward McManus)

University Air Squadrons – Training squadrons were established at Cambridge and Oxford universities in 1925 and at London 10 years later. From September 1938 it became compulsory for UAS members to join the RAF or a direct entry reserve, after leaving university.

Almost 100 former UAS members earned the Battle of Britain clasp.

Vector – A course to follow.

"On the 13th August the Squadron was scrambled and vectored to intercept a large formation of bombers expected to cross the coast in the vicinity of Rye at 20,000ft." Gp Capt Tom Dalton-Morgan recalling his time with No 43 Squadron in *Tommy Leader*.

Victoria Cross – Britain's highest award for gallantry. Instituted on January 29 1856 when Queen Victoria signed a Royal Warrant. Some awards were backdated to the Crimean War.

The only VC ever won by Fighter Command was earned on August 16, by Flt Lt James Brindley Eric Nicolson of No 249 Squadron, which had moved south to Boscombe Down from Church Fenton two days previously.

Just after 1pm on the 16th "Nick" Nicolson was leading the squadron's Red Section, which also consisted of Plt Off Martyn King and Sqn Ldr Eric King, flying as a supernumerary. Nicolson spotted three enemy aircraft near Gosport and was about to attack them when Spitfires intervened. Red Section was then bounced by German fighters and all three Hurricanes were hit.

Nicolson was wounded in the foot and his reserve tank was set on fire. He started to bale out, but then opened fire on a Bf 110 that flew in front of him. After he left the aircraft, with severe burns, he was hit by pellets from a shotgun fired by a Home Guard soldier. He landed in Millbrook, Southampton, where a doctor and nurse, who happened to be nearby, were quickly on the scene. Nicolson dictated to Nurse Edna Brown (or, according to another account, to PC Eric Coleman) a telegram to his wife Muriel which read, "Shot down. Very slightly hurt. Full particulars later. All my love Nick." In fact his injuries were so severe that for a time he was not expected to live.

Sqn Ldr King brought his damaged aircraft back to Boscombe Down, but Plt Off King baled out. Although his parachute opened, it subsequently collapsed and he died after falling into the garden of a house at Shirley, Southampton. It is possible that his parachute had been hit by fire from the ground.

In September No 249 Squadron moved to North Weald. On October 26, Wg Cdr Victor Beamish, the station's OC, signed a recommendation for a DFC for Nicolson for his actions on August 16. Two days later AVM Park added his remarks as AOC, which concluded, "For this outstanding act of gallantry and magnificent display of fighting spirit, I recommend this officer for the immediate award of the Victoria Cross." On November 3 Park's recommendation was endorsed by Air Chf Mshl Dowding. The award was gazetted on November 15.

Nicolson was then at the Palace Hotel, Torquay, which was being used as a convalescent home for RAF officers. He seems to have been dismayed to be singled out amongst Fighter Command airman and sent another telegram to his wife in which he said, "Just got VC. Don't know why."

It is now clear that the indirect intervention of the King played a large part in the award. On August 29 Air Mshl Gossage, Air Member for Personnel, had sent a letter to senior RAF figures in which he drew attention to a conversation between the King and Sir Archibald Sinclair, Secretary of State for Air, in which His Majesty had expressed surprise, "that the recent exploits of the Royal Air Force had not produced more recommendations for awards of the Victoria Cross."

From August 1943 Nicolson commanded No 27 Squadron, operating Mosquitos in Burma. He was awarded the DFC a year later. On May 2 1945, while serving on the staff of RAF HQ Burma, Wg Cdr Nicolson flew as an observer on a bombing sortie in a Liberator of No 355 Squadron. The aircraft came down in the sea and he was not amongst the survivors.

Victoria Station Dornier – Shortly after midday on September 15 (later Battle of Britain Day) part of a Dornier Do 17Z hit the forecourt of London's Victoria Station. Other wreckage fell on a building in Vauxhall Bridge Road. At much the same time a Hurricane from No 504 Squadron, based at Hendon, crashed in Buckingham Palace Road, with the pilot, Sgt Ray Holmes, landing by parachute in Hugh Street, Pimlico.

From that day these highly public incidents have become some of the most discussed of the Battle. Intriguingly, the

Flt Lt James Nicolson (centre) shortly after he had been told that he was to receive the Victoria Cross. He was still recovering from his wounds at the Palace Hotel, Torquay, which was being used as an RAF convalescent home. (Courtesy Imperial War Museum, London, negative number CH 1700)

diversity of accounts of the circumstances has been considerable.

Writing in the 1980s (in *The Battle of Britain Then and Now*), the historian, Peter Cornwell, suggested that the aircraft most responsible for the demise of the Dornier was a Hurricane flown by Flt Lt Jerrard Jefferies, commanding B Flight of No 310 Squadron. Cornwell listed several other fighters that attacked the German, a straggler through engine trouble. He credited Holmes with being the last to attack and with reporting that his wing had struck something during the attack.

One more recent account claimed that, "Sgt Ray Holmes, his ammunition exhausted, heroically rammed a German Dornier bomber heading resolutely towards Buckingham Palace."

Some members of the crew of the Dornier evacuated the aircraft. The pilot, Oberleutnant Robert Zehbe, landed in Kennington, where he was attacked by civilians, some of whom were claimed by witnesses to be shouting, "Kill him, kill him". He was rescued by soldiers, but died of his injuries.

Pilots of No. 310 (Czecho-Slovak) Squadron in front of Hawker Hurricane Mk I, P3143 NN-D, (NN was the Squadron's code) at Duxford. Sitting fifth from the left is Flt Lt Jerrard Jefferies who attacked the "Victoria Station Dornier". He later changed his name to Latimer and was lost, as a Sqn Ldr, on April 15 1943, flying as an observer in a Lancaster of No 106 Squadron. The aircraft crashed in France, while returning from a raid on Stuttgart. (Courtesy of Imperial War Museum, London, negative no CH 1299)

Weaver's (also referred to as Tail End, or Arse End, Charlie) – One or two aircraft positioned above and behind the rest of a fighter squadron to watch for enemy fighters.

Women's Auxiliary Air Force – The Force was established in June 1939 with the aim of freeing men for operational roles. Its members became known as "WAAFs". Previously the Women's Royal Air Force had existed briefly at the end of the First World War. This name was used again from 1949, when the WAAF was re-formed and, in 1994, the women's service became fully integrated into the RAF.

Much comment was passed about the desirability or otherwise of placing women in roles traditionally carried out by men, such as in control rooms. Dowding and Watson-Watt both pressed for the use of WAAFs at chain home stations. The doubters featured alleged lack of stamina and inability to cope under fire, as well as exposure to bad language, amongst their concerns.

The reality proved different as is evidenced by some of the awards made in 1940. In May, Cpl Daphne Pearson, at the Coastal Command station at Detling, Kent, dragged the badly injured pilot of a crashed Anson clear of the burning wreckage and shielded him as bombs exploded. She was awarded the EGM, later converted to the GC.

During the Battle of Britain, MMs were earned by Sgt Elizabeth Mortimer, Sgt Helen Turner and Cpl Elspeth Henderson (at Biggin Hill), Sgt Jean Youle and Cpl Josephine

Robins (Detling) and Cpl Avis Hearn (Poling, Sussex, chain home station).

"Because I had a lot of plots to send and I love my country." Mrs Avis Parsons MM explaining why, as Cpl Hearn, she ignored the order to take cover as a large enemy force approached Poling on August 18.

"Yes that is the ribbon of the MM and, yes, apparently women can win it." The standard reply given by Mrs Parsons to puzzled soldiers who approached her during the war.

"My major memory of 1940 is of the young WAAFs who endured the bombing of the aerodromes such as Biggin Hill and Kenley and carried on at their posts with great bravery." Sqn Ldr Tony Pickering, a Hurricane pilot in the Battle.

"I really do not know why I have been given the Military Medal, as I only did what everyone else would have done.

These WAAFs and airmen at the Chain Home Station above Ventnor on the Isle of Wight could hardly have been more in the front line. The photograph was taken during the Battle. (Courtesy Imperial War Museum, London, negative no, C 1868)

Across the road from Biggin Hill airfield, in the area that formerly housed the RAF married quarters, are roads named after the three WAAFs who won the MM in the Battle. Sergeant Mortimer was sometimes known as Elizabeth. The date is that on which the award was gazetted.

The actual raid was a lightning one; we saw the German planes coming and at first thought they were our own as they were so very low, then we made for the nearest shelter as the bombs rained down on us. Two of us were literally blown into the dug-out by the blast of a bomb which burst just behind us, and the next nearly blew us out again as it was a direct hit on the shelter, killing four men and injuring others.

"We helped some out of the dug-out which was full of awful dust and fumes from the explosion, and got a stretcher for a seriously injured man...

"The morning after the raid we turned into carpenter and demolition squads, as each section had to make the building habitable. The roof of ours was decidedly impaired so we climbed up to investigate, and were forced into a perilous slide to the ground every time the siren sounded or there were signs of air activity overhead."

Extracts from a radio script prepared for Cpl Josie Robins MM.

BIBLIOGRAPHY

Among the publications and documents that were consulted in compiling this dictionary were:

Air Chief Marshal Dowding's despatch, 'The Battle of Britain, August 1941' and supplement to the *London Gazette*, September 1946

A Brief History of Civil Defence: Edited by Tim Essex-Lopresti, Civil Defence Association, 2005

A Clasp for 'The Few': Kenneth G Wynn, published by the author, 1981

Ack Ack: Britain's Defence Against Air Attack in the Second World War: Sir Frederick Pile Bt, George G Harrap & Co, 1949

Air Defence: Major General E B Ashmore, Longmans, Green & Co, 1929

Air Defence of Great Britain: John R Busby, Ian Allan, 1973

A Lighter Shade of Blue: Christopher Foxley-Norris, Ian Allan, 1978

Battle of Britain Day: Alfred Price, Sidgwick & Jackson, 1990

Battle of Britain: The Hardest Day 18 August 1940: Alfred Price, Book Club Associates 1979

Battle over Britain: Francis K Mason, Aston Publications, 2nd edition 1990

Beyond the Call of Duty: Brian James Crabb, Shaun Tyas, 2006

Big Wing: the biography of Air Chief Marshal Sir Trafford Leigh-Mallory, B N Dunn, Airlife Publishing, 1992

Billy Drake, Fighter Leader: Group Captain B Drake with Christopher Shores, Grub Street, 2002

British Gallantry Awards: P E Abbott and J M A Tamplin, Guinness Superlatives, 1971

Churchill: Roy Jenkins, Macmillan, 2001

Clouds of Fear: Roger Hall, Bailey Brothers & Swinfen, 1975

Dictionary of National Biography: various entries on line

Dowding and Headquarters Fighter Command: Peter Flint, Airlife Publishing, 1996

Dowding and the Battle of Britain: Robert Wright, Military Book Society edition, 1969

Dowding of Fighter Command: Victor of the Battle of Britain: Vincent Orange, Grub Street, 2008

Enemy Coast Ahead: Guy Gibson, Goodall Publications, 1986 edition

Fighter Command Losses of the Second World War, vol 1, 1939-41: Norman L R Franks, Midland Publishing, 1997

Fireman at War: Neil Wallington, David & Charles, 1981

First Light: Geoffrey Wellum, Viking, 2002

Fleet Air Arm: John Moore, Chapman and Hall, 1943

Flying Fever: AVM S F Vincent, Jarrolds, 1972

For Gallantry: Kenneth Hare-Scott, Peter Garnett, 1951

For Valour – The Air VCs: Chaz Bowyer, Grub Street, 1992

From Dogfight to Diplomacy: Donald MacDonell, Edited by Lois MacDonell and Anne Mackay, Pen & Sword, 2005.

Green Two, Sgt Dennis Noble: Keith Arnold, Southern Counties Aviation Research/Publications, 2003.

Harvest of Messerscmitts: Dennis Knight, Frederick Warne, 1981

High Commanders of the Royal Air Force: Air Commodore Henry Probert, HMSO, 1991

London at War 1939-45: Philip Ziegler, Sinclair-Stevenson, 1995

Lonely Warrior: Jean Offenberg, edited by Victor Houart, Souvenir Press, 1956

Men of the Battle of Britain: Kenneth G Wynn, CCB Associates, 2nd edition, 1999

One of The Few: Gp Capt J A Kent, William Kimber, 1971

One of The Few: John Shipman, Pen & Sword, 2008

Partners in Blue: Katharine Bentley Beauman, Hutchinson, 1971

RAF Biggin Hill: Graham Wallace, Putnam & Co, 1969

RAF Fighter Command: Norman Franks, Patrick Stephens, 1992

RAF Kenley: Peter Flint, Terence Dalton, 1985

RAF Squadrons: Wing Commander C G Jefford, Airlife Publishing, 2001

Reach For the Sky: Paul Brickhill, Fontana Books edition, 1957

Royal Air Force Bomber Command Losses of the Second World War: (particularly vol 1), 1939-40: W R Chorley, Midland Counties Publications, 1992

Sailor Malan: Oliver Walker, Cassell Co, 1953

Shot Down in Flames: Geoffrey Page, Grub Street edition, 1999

Sir Keith Park: Vincent Orange, Methuen 1984

Some of the Few: John P M Reid, Macdonald, 1960

Special Correspondent: Jean Stroud, Ward Lock, 1969

Stapme: David Ross, Grub Street, 2002

Target England: Derek Wood, Jane's Publishing Company, 1980

That Eternal Summer: Ralph Barker, Collins, 1990

The Battle of Britain: Edward Bishop, George Allen & Unwin, 1960

The Battle of Britain: HMSO, 1941

The Battle of Britain Then and Now: edited by Winston G Ramsey, Battle of Britain Prints International, 1980

The Battle of France Then and Now: Peter D Cornwell, Battle of Britain Prints International, 2007

The Battle Re-thought: Edited by Air Commodore Henry Probert and Sebastian Cox, Royal Air Force Historical Society, 1991

The Blitz Then and Now: Edited by Winston Ramsey, Battle of Britain Prints International, three volumes from 1987

The Burning Blue: Edited by Paul Addison and Jeremy A Crang, Pimlico, 2000

The Chancellors: Roy Jenkins, Macmillan, 1998

The Defence of London 1915-1918: A Rawlinson, Andrew Melrose, 1923

The Fated Sky: Sir Philip Joubert de la Ferte, White Lion edition, 1977

The Flying Sword: Tom Moulson, Macdonald, 1964

The Hamlyn Concise Guide to British Aircraft of World War II: David Mondey, Chancellor Press, 1994

The Holy Fox, A Life of Lord Halifax: Andrew Roberts, George Weidenfeld & Nicolson, 1991

The London Blitz – A Fireman's Tale: Cyril Demarne, Battle of Britain Prints International, 1991

The Narrow Margin: Derek Wood and Derek Dempster, Hutchinson, 1961 and later editions

The Right of the Line: John Terraine, Hodder and Stoughton, 1985

The Second World War, Vol II, Their Finest Hour: Winston S Churchill, Cassell & Co, 1949

The Source Book of the RAF: Ken Delve, Airlife Publishing, 1994

Tommy Leader: Group Captain Tom Dalton-Morgan with Clive Williams, Griffon International, 2007

Twenty-one Squadrons: Leslie Hunt, Crecy Books edition, 1992

War & Society: University of New South Wales, various issues

Westminster in War: William Sansom, Faber and Faber, 1947

Who Won the Battle of Britain?: H R Allen, DFC, Panther Books, 1976

With Wings Like Eagles: Michael Korda, Harper, 2009

Women in Air Force Blue: Squadron Leader Beryl E Escott, Patrick Stephens/Thorsons Publishing, 1989

Files consulted at the National Archive included:-

AIR 2/3115 - Women's Auxiliary Air Force: Formation of WAAF

AIR 2/6557 - Memorials (code B, 49): Battle of Britain Roll of Honour, RAF Chapel, Westminster Abbey

AIR 2/7281 - Royal Air Force Fighter Command (Code B, 67/12) Tactics against German mass formations 1940

AIR 2/7771 - Enemy air offensive against Great Britain (Code B,45): Battle of Britain: Sir Hugh Dowding's despatch

AIR 2/9455 - Women's Auxiliary Air Force: WAAF recruiting personnel: war establishment

AIR 6/75 - Air Council Minutes - Jan 1944 to Dec 1945

AIR 8/262 - Department of the Chief of the Air Staff: Action arising from War Conferences

AIR 8/272 - Department of the Chief of the Air Staff: employment in France

AIR 8/276 - Department of the Chief of the Air Staff: Air staff requirements in aircraft

AIR 8/287 - Department of the Chief of the Air Staff: Air support for France 1939/40

AIR 8/354 - Department of the Chief of the Air Staff: allocation of British Air Forces in France 1939/40

AIR 8/480 - Department of the Chief of Air Staff: Division of responsibilities between Air Ministry & Min of Aircraft Production: negotiations with Lord Beaverbrook

AIR 16/672 - Proposed roll of honour for pilots engaged in the Battle of Britain - August 1942 to February 1943

AIR 16/887 - WAAF Historical Records 1940 June - 1942 December

AIR 20/4200 - Battle of Britain: commemoration 1942 March to 1945 July

AIR 27 - Air Ministry and successors: Operation Records Books, Squadrons

AIR 28/345 - Hawkinge ORB - July 1935 to November 1945

AIR 28/512 - Manston ORB - 1916 to 1941

AIR 35/47 - Air staff notes on Air Council meetings

CAB 79 - War Cabinet Chiefs of Staff Minutes and Memoranda